Celebrity KNITTING

Celebrity KNITTING

KATHARINE HADLEY AND JANE PROCTER
PHOTOGRAPHS BY CHRISTOPHER MOORE

This edition produced exclusively for
WHSMITH

Yarns and Patterns supplied by
Patons & Baldwins Limited

Design and Technical Adviser
Sandra Cook

Photographs
Christopher Moore
Additional Photographs
Nick Briggs (Three Degrees) and Martin Lawrence (Julie Walters, Audrey Eyton, Bonnie Langford)

Editor
Jane Olliver
Assistant Editor
Nan Froman

Design
Millions Design

First published in 1985 by
Grisewood & Dempsey Limited
Elsley Court, 20-22 Great Titchfield Street
London W1P 7AD

Phototypeset by the Letterbox Company, Woking and Signal Communications, London.
Colour separations by Newsele Litho Ltd, Milan, Italy
Printed and bound in Portugal by Printer Portuguesa
ISBN 0 906279 34 8

ACKNOWLEDGEMENTS
The publishers and authors wish to thank Patons & Baldwins and their wonderful team of knitters, without whose co-operation this book would not have been possible. We would particularly like to thank Ron Irons who agreed to the collaboration, and Sandra Cook who most generously gave design and technical advice.

We would also like to thank the following hairdressers, make-up artists and suppliers.

Lysette Anthony: Hair and make-up by Nigel Herbert. **Debi Brett:** Jewellery by Butler & Wilson. **Children:** Pale denim jeans from Fenwicks. **Sharron Davies:** Hair and make-up by Nigel Herbert. Jewellery from Fenwicks. **Kiki Dee:** Hair and make-up by Nigel Herbert. Jewellery from Harvey Nichols. **Angela Douglas:** Make-up by Lyn at Cosmetics à la Carte. Hair by Ross at John Frieda at the Ritz. Lalique style jewellery and grey pearls from Harvey Nichols. Bracelet with bow from Van Peterson, 117 Walton Street, London SW3. Belt by Osprey Co. Shoes by Principles. **Diane Fletcher:** Trousers from Jaeger. **Kate Garner:** Jewellery by Sheila Teague. **Clare Grogan:** Hair and make-up by Allister Logue. Red boots from Faith. Earrings and bangles from Adrien Mann. Tights by Christian Dior at Selfridges. **Polly Hemingway:** Hair by Peter Forrester for Schumi. Make-up by Theresa Fairminer. Jewellery by Carolynne Read. **Gary Holton:** Leather trousers from General Leather Company. Sunglasses by Alaia from Browns. **Hot Gossip:** Photographed at Chelsea Dance Studios. Hair by Heidi at Smile. Dance accessories from Pineapple Dance Centre. **Geraldine James:** Hair by Mitch at Schumi. Make-up by Maudie James. Jumpsuit by Plantation. Jewellery by Butler & Wilson. **Jilly Johnson:** Tights from The Sock Shop. **Bonnie Langford:** Gloves and jewellery from Miss Selfridge. Ski pants from Harvey Nichols. **Molly Parkin:** Jewellery by Andrew Logan. **Tim Pigott-Smith:** Trousers from Austin Reed. **Eve Pollard:** Make-up by Nigel Herbert. **David Shilling:** Grooming by Allister Logue. **Three Degrees:** Hair by Richard Field of Fields Salon, 128 Crawford Street, London W1. Make-up by Paula Owen. Jewellery from Butler & Wilson and Fenwicks. **Julie Walters:** Jewellery by Butler & Wilson. **Robert White:** Trousers from Ixiz. **Susannah York:** hair by Annie Russell of Annie Russell, 1 Kensington Church Walk, London W8.

CONTENTS

INTRODUCTION

There is a great pleasure to be found in beautifully knitted things, and with the wealth of colour and new yarns available to us today, any woman, or man, can look elegant no matter how small their clothes budget.

At the designer end of the market of course, garments can cost a great deal. Today in the 1980s, in New York, Paris, Milan and London, Jackie Onassis or the Princess of Wales may pay £200 for a hand knit that, in truth, most of us could make for a fraction of the cost.

Few of us can afford such prices. Yet those great names in knitwear design, Missoni, Sonia Rykiel, Marion Foale and the Princess of Wales' designer Sasha Kagan, have done all of us an enormous favour. They have shown us the flexibility of yarn and shape. They have done what great fashion houses must always do if they are to survive – give inspiration and demonstrate what we can do ourselves.

Designers make their clothes for men and women with rather more perfect bodies than most of us. Jane Procter and I wanted to produce a set of designs to flatter ordinary people, and to go with their daily needs.

The book was a pleasure to put together because of the very real enthusiasm shown by the personalities who so kindly helped design and model the garments.

Together with Sandra Cook of Patons, we discussed their favourite colours, their life styles and their best and worst features. We came up with ideas that look good on them and we hope will look good on many more people.

Our pleasure was enriched by theirs in having something especially made for them – a feeling that will be familiar to all expert knitters and one to be discovered by those who have only just decided to try their hand.

We were particularly interested to discover that the men were prepared to spend exactly the same amount of time and trouble on their designs as the women. And they were just as interested in the colours and textures of yarn.

Tim Pigott-Smith, the unobliging policeman in *Jewel In The Crown*, produced an attractive, clean-lined sweater for men with three different sleeve lengths, ingenious in all temperatures. Roy Marsden, usually impeccably turned out on television as the devastating Inspector Dalgliesh, made a point of choosing the comfortable sort of big knitted top for messing about in that most men adore.

David Gower, England's cricket captain, smartly avoided any overtly sporty lines to his sweater.

American singer, Robert White, chose a collar to protect the beloved voice. Gary Holton of *Auf Wiedersehen Pet*, picked a tough looking rocker top that should please the haughtiest teenager. And Patrick Hughes, the painter of international renown, who is nearly as famous on both sides of the Atlantic for his elegance as his work, designed a star-studded sweater that can take a man anywhere.

We were particularly lucky to have international hat and clothing designer David Shilling draw up, exclusively for this book, a classic head-turning, entrance maker.

The hand of another famous designer is also evident here. Barbara Hulanicki, the woman who made Biba dominant in fashion in the 60s has designed a white suit that will flatter a woman to perdition. It makes slender what is not, flatters legs that are less than perfect and the wide shoulders make a frame for a pretty face.

Geraldine James, of *Jewel In The Crown* fame, has also picked a garment that will streamline.

Jane Procter and I feel that this wide range of designs for all occasions will provide eye-catching garments for every kind of taste.

We would like to thank our celebrities for their imagination, and patience and in particular the children who kindly agreed to give us their time: Katie Corcoran, Dido Xenakis, Hannah Nana, Lucy Johnson, Jamie Lawson, Luke Wilson and my two sons Thomas Hope and Hugh Sington.

Clare Grogan

BARE MIDRIFF MIDI SUIT

Clare Grogan first made her name when she starred in *Gregory's Girl* – Bill Forsyth's film of awakening passion in a comprehensive school. She went on to become a successful pop star with the group *Altered Images* and then returned to Bill Forsyth in his movie *Comfort and Joy.* You have to be slender to look good in this dashing, vividly coloured, off-the-waist midi with its Japanese influenced boxy top.

MATERIALS

Patons Beehive DK

Skirt	Main shade (**M**)	**50 g. balls**	6	6	7
	Contrast (**C**)	**50 g. balls**	1	1	1
Top	Main shade (**M**)	**50 g. balls**	3	4	4
	Contrast (**C**)	**50 g. balls**	2	3	3

Pair Milward needles each Nos. 8 (4 mm), 9 (3¾ mm) and 10 (3¼ mm).

MEASUREMENTS

Skirt, to fit hips	**cm.**	86	91	97
	in.	34	36	38
Length, allowing for waistband to be rolled over twice	**cm.**	74	74	74
	in.	29	29	29
Top, to fit bust	**cm.**	81	86	91
	in.	32	34	36
Actual width around underarms	**cm.**	107	112	117
	in.	42	44	46
Length from shoulder	**cm.**	36	36	37
	in.	14	14	14½

TENSION

22 sts. and 30 rows to 10 cm. (4 in.) over stocking stitch on No. 8 (4 mm) needles.

ABBREVIATIONS

k., knit; **p.**, purl; **M.**, main shade; **C.**, contrast; **sts.**, stitches; **st.st.**, stocking st.; **g.st.**, garter st.; **m.1**, make 1 by picking up and knitting into back of horizontal strand lying before next st.; **dec.**, decrease, decreasing; **tog.**, together; **t.b.l.**, through back of loops; **beg.**, beginning; **alt.**, alternate; **rep.**, repeat; **cm.**, centimetres; **in.**, inches.

SKIRT

Front and back (2 pieces alike)

With No. 10 (3¼mm) needles and C, cast on 110 (116; 122) sts.
Work 14 rows in g.st.
Next row: K. 5 (8; 11), (m.1, k. 9) 11 times, m.1, k. to end. 122 (128; 134) sts.
Break C. Join in M.
Change to No. 8 (4 mm) needles and beg. k. row work in st.st. for 22 rows.
Shape thus:–
Dec. row: K. 20 (22; 24), k. 2 tog. t.b.l., k. 4, k. 2 tog., k. *to last* 28 (30; 32) sts., k. 2 tog. t.b.l., k. 4, k. 2 tog., k. to end. (4 sts. decreased).
Work 29 rows straight.
Rep. these 30 rows until 102 (108; 114) sts. remain.
Work straight until skirt measures 59 cm. (23¼ in.), ending after a p. row and dec. 6 (4; 6) sts. evenly on last row. 96 (104; 108) sts.
Change to No. 10 (3¼ mm) needles and rib thus:–
1st row: K. 3, (p. 2, k. 2) to last st., k. 1.
2nd row: K. 1, (p. 2, k. 2) to last 3 sts., p. 2, k. 1.
Rep. these 2 rows for 12 cm. (4¾ in.), ending after a 1st row.
Next row: P. thus forming a ridge on wrong side.
Beg. 1st row work 8 rows in rib again.
Next row: K. thus forming a ridge on wrong side.
Beg. 1st row, thus reversing rib for top of roll-over waistband, continue in rib for a further 7 cm. (3 in.). Cast off *loosely* in rib.

TO MAKE UP

Do not press. Join side seams. Press seams. Roll over top of ribbing 2 or 3 times to right side.

TOP

Front

With No. 10 (3¼ mm) needles and C, cast on 115 (121; 127) sts.
Work 14 rows in g.st.
Next row: K. 2 (5; 8), (m.1, k. 8) 14 times, m.1, k. to end. 130 (136; 142) sts.
Break C. Join in M.
Change to No. 8 (4 mm) needles and beg. k. row work in st.st. until front measures 28 cm. (11 in.) from beg., ending after a p. row.
Shape neck thus:–
Next row: K. 43 (45; 47), in turn. Continue on this group. Dec. 1 st. at neck edge on next 5 rows. 38 (40; 42) sts.
Continue straight until work measures 36 (36; 37) cm., 14 (14; 14½) in. from beg., ending at side edge.
Shape shoulder by casting off 9 (10; 10) sts. at beg. of next and 2 following alt. rows.
Work 1 row. Cast off.
With right side facing, slip centre 44 (46; 48) sts. on a spare needle. Rejoin M and k. 1 row.
Complete as first half.

Back

Work as front but working 8 more rows before shaping neck.

Sleeves

With No. 8 (4 mm) needles and C, cast on 95 (100; 105) sts.
Work in g.st. for 14 cm. (5½ in.). Cast off.

Neckband

First join left shoulder. With No. 8 (4 mm) needles and C, right side facing, k. up 15 (15; 18) sts. down left back neck, k. across centre sts., k. up 15 (15; 18) sts. up right back neck, 21 (21; 24) sts. down left front neck, k. across centre sts., finally k. up 21 (21; 24) sts. up right front neck. 160 (164; 180) sts.
Work 4 rows in g.st.
Change to No. 9 (3¾ mm) needles and work 5 rows in g.st.
Change to No. 10 (3¼ mm) needles and work 5 more rows in g.st. Cast off.

TO MAKE UP

Do not press. Join right shoulder and neckband. Allowing approximately 72 (76; 80) rows for armhole stitch cast-off edges of sleeves in postition to back and front yoke. Join side and sleeve seams.

David Shilling

COLOUR BLOCKED SWEATER

David Shilling, international hatter and dress designer, models his flamboyant colour blocked sweater which guarantees that any man or woman who wears it steals the show. His best designs are already collections at London's Victoria and Albert Museum and New York's Metropolitan Museum. This one could be your collector's item.

A	(Patons Cotton Top Shade 6400)	**50 g. balls**	15
B	(Patons Focus on Cotton Shade 2095)	**25 g. balls**	2
C	(Patons Solo Chunky Shade 2235)	**50 g. balls**	1
D	(Patons Cotton Ribbon Shade 2107)	**50 g. balls**	1
E	(Patons Focus on Cotton Shade 2097)	**25 g. balls**	2
F	(Patons Mohair Focus Shade 2042)	**25 g. balls**	1
G	(Patons Cotton Ribbon Shade 2100)	**50 g. balls**	1
H	(Patons Mohair Focus Shade 2046)	**25 g. balls**	1
J	(Patons Solo Chunky Shade 2230)	**50 g. balls**	1
K	(Patons Moorland D.K. Shade 6588)	**50 g. balls**	2
L	(Patons Solo Chunky Shade 2023)	**50 g. balls**	1
M	(Patons Mohair Focus Shade 2050)	**25 g. balls**	1
N	(Patons Diana Shade 9230)	**50 g. balls**	1
P	(Patons Mohair Focus Shade 2078)	**25 g. balls**	2
R	(Patons Solo Chunky Shade 2216)	**50 g. balls**	1
S	(Patons Cotton Ribbon Shade 2112)	**50 g. balls**	1
T	(Patons Mohair Focus Shade 2066)	**25 g. balls**	1

Pair each No. 6 (5 mm) and No. 3 (6½ mm) Knitting needles

MEASUREMENTS
One size to fit bust/chest 86-107 cm. (34-42 in.)
Length approx. 70 cm. (27½ in.)

TENSION
14.5 sts. and 20 rows to 10 cm. (4 in.) measured over st.st. on No. 3 (6½ mm) needles using A double.

ABBREVIATIONS
k., knit; **p.**, purl; **sts.**, stitches; **st.st.**, stocking stitch; **tog.**, together; **inc.**, increase; **dec.**, decrease; **beg.**, beginning; **alt.**, alternate; **rep.**, repeat; **patt.**, pattern; **cont.**, continue; **foll.**, following; **rem.**, remaining; **r.s.**, right side; **w.s.**, wrong side; **cm.**, centimetres; **mm.**, millimetres; **in.**, inches.

NOTES
2 strands of A are used tog. throughout design.
2 strands of K are used tog. throughout design.
When working in patt. from chart, use separate balls of yarn for each section, twisting yarns on w.s. to avoid a hole. Place markers on work where indicated.
For front: Read odd rows of chart k. from right to left and even rows p. from left to right;
For back: Read odd rows of chart k. from left to right and even rows p. from right to left;
MB = Make bobble as follows: Make a loop in appropriate colour and place on left hand needle, k. 1, p. 1, k. 1, p. 1, k. 1 into loop, (turn, p. 5, turn k. 5) twice, turn, pass 2nd, 3rd, 4th and 5th sts. over 1st st. and fasten off bobble.

FRONT
With No. 3 (6½ mm) needles and A, cast on 26 sts. and work in st.st. for 10 cm. (4 in.) ending with r.s. facing.
Shape underarm by inc. 1 st. at beg. of next and every foll. 4th row until there are 39 sts. Work 3 rows.
Now inc. 1 st. at beg. of next and every foll. alt. row until there are 70 sts., ending with r.s. facing.
Cast on 5 sts. at beg. of next and foll. 3 alt. rows. (90 sts.)
Work 1 row, thus ending with r.s. facing.
Now work straight foll. patt. on chart for 92 rows.
Keeping patt. on chart correct, shape underarm by casting off 5 sts. at beg. of next and foll. 3 alt rows. Work 1 row. (70 sts.)
Now dec. 1 st. at beg. of next and every foll. alt. row until 39 sts. rem., ending with r.s. facing.
Dec. 1 st. at beg. of next and every foll. 4th row

26 pattern stitches

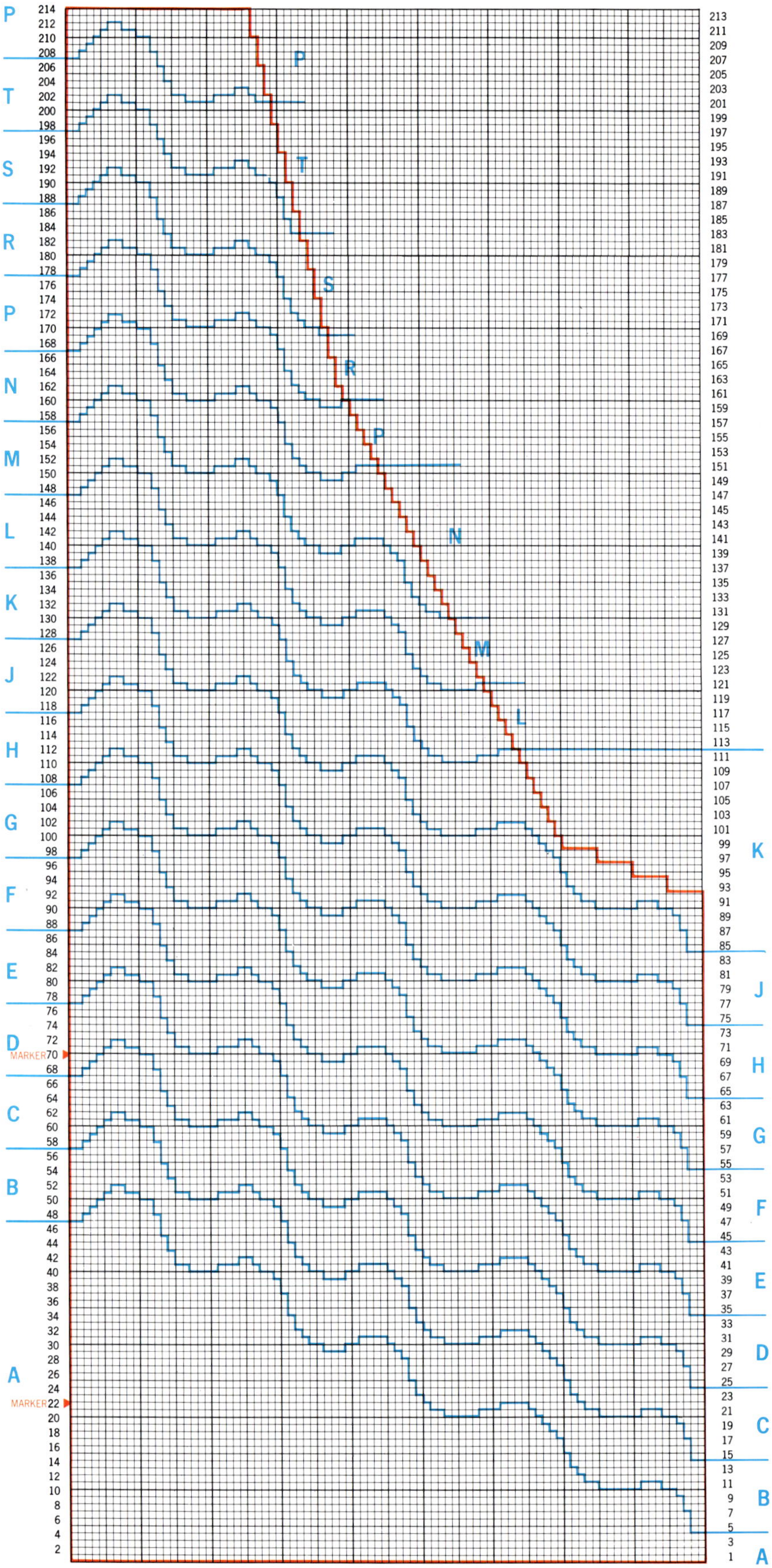

90 pattern stitches

until 26 sts. rem. Work 3 rows.
Cont. in p., in st.st. for 10 cm. (4 in.) more. Cast off.

BACK
Work as for Front, reversing shapings and chart.

MAKE UP AND BORDERS
Do not press. Join right shoulder to markers.
Neck border: With r.s. facing, No. 6 (5 mm) needles and A, knit up 36 sts. between markers on front and 36 sts. between markers on back. (72 sts.)
Work in k. 1, p. 1 rib for 7 cm. (2¾ in.).
Using a No. 3 (6½ mm) needle, cast off loosely in rib.
Join left shoulder and neck border.
Fold neck border in half to w.s. and slip-hem loosely in position.
Right wrist cuff: With r.s. facing, No. 6 (5 mm) needles and A, Knit up 52 sts. along lower edge of right sleeve.
Next row: P. 3, p. 2 tog., (p. 2, p. 2 tog.) 11 times, p. 3. (40 sts.)
Work in k. 1, p. 1 rib for 8 cm. (3 in.).
Cast off neatly in rib.
Left wrist cuff: Work as for right wrist cuff using P in place of A.
Lower edge ribs: With r.s. facing, No. 6 (5 mm) needles and P, knit up 92 sts. along lower edge on front.
Next row: (p. 1, p. 2 tog.) 6 times, (p. 2, p. 2 tog.) 13 times, (p. 1, p. 2 tog.) 7 times, p. 1. (66 sts.)
Work in k. 1, p.1 rib for 8 cm. (3 in.).
Cast off neatly in rib.
Rep. along lower edge on Back.
Bobbles: Using No. 3 (6½ mm) needles, make bobbles in each colour.
Randomly sew bobbles to garment as in photograph.
Make tassels in each colour and attach to garment as in photograph.

Patti Boulaye

BACKLESS, PUFFED SLEEVE MIDI

Singer Patti Boulaye is one of Prince Charles's favourite artists. Frequently seen on TV chat shows, she is happily married and has two children. Patti has chosen this glamorous cream dress to match the drama of her own good looks.

MATERIALS					
Patons Cotton Perle	**50 g. balls**	17	17	18	18
Pair Milward needles each Nos. 9 (3¾ mm) and 11 (3 mm).					
15 buttons.					
MEASUREMENTS					
To fit bust	**cm.**	81	86	91	97
	in.	32	34	36	38
Length from shoulder	**cm.**	102	103	104	105
	in.	40	40½	41	41½
Sleeve seam	**cm.**	44	44	44	44
	in.	17½	17½	17½	17½

TENSION
24 sts. and 30 rows to 10 cm. (4 in.) over rib (when stretched) on No. 9 (3¾ mm) needles.

ABBREVIATIONS
k., knit; **p.**, purl; **sts.**, stitches; **sl.**, slip; **tog.**, together; **p.s.s.o.**, pass slipped st. over; **inc.**, increase, increasing; **m.1**, make 1 by picking up and knitting into back of horizontal thread lying before next st.; **dec.**, decrease, decreasing; **beg.**, beginning; **alt.**, alternate; **rep.**, repeat; **cm.**, centimetres; **in.**, inches.

RIGHT HALF OF BACK
With No. 9 (3¾ mm) needles, cast on 63 (65; 69; 71) sts.
1st row: K. 2, (p. 1, k. 1) to last st., k. 1.
2nd row: K. 1, (p.1, k. 1) to end.
Work 18 more rows in rib.**
Shape skirt thus:
Dec. row: Rib 25, sl. 1, k. 2 tog., p.s.s.o., rib to end. (2 sts. decreased).
Work 19 rows straight.
Rep. the last 20 rows until 41 (49; 53; 55) sts. remain.
***Work straight until back measures 64 cm. (25 in.) from beg., ending after a 2nd rib row.
Shape 'V' neck slope thus:
Keeping rib correct, dec. 1 st. at end of next row and at same edge on every following 5th row until 35 (37; 41; 43) sts. remain, thus ending with right side facing for next row.***
Shape armhole, still shaping 'V' neck thus:
Next row: Cast off 5 (5; 5; 5) sts., rib to end.
Next row: Rib to end.
****Decreasing 1 st. at neck edge on every 5th row from previous neck decrease, at the same time dec. 1 st. at armhole edge on next 3 rows, then on the 2 (3; 4; 5) following alt. rows. 24 (24; 27; 27) sts.
N.B.: 10 (11; 12; 13) sts. in all decreased at armhole edge.
Continue dec. at neck edge only on every 5th row from previous dec. until 17 (18; 19; 20) sts. remain.
Work straight until back measures 19 (20; 21; 23) cm., 7½ (8; 8½; 9) in. from beg. of armhole shaping.
Cast off in rib.

LEFT HALF OF BACK
Work as right half of back to **.
Shape skirt thus:
Dec. row: Rib to last 28 sts., k. 3 tog., rib to end
Work 19 rows straight.
Rep. the last 20 rows until 47 (49; 53; 55) sts. remain.
Work as right half from *** to ***, reversing shapings.
Work 1 row straight.
Shape armhole, still shaping 'V' neck thus:
Next row: Cast off 5 (5; 5; 5) sts., rib to end.
Complete as right half working from ****to end.

FRONT
With No. 9 (3¾ mm) needles, cast on 129 (135; 141; 147) sts.
Work 20 rows in rib as on back.
Shape skirt thus:
Dec. row: Rib 25, sl. 1, k. 2 tog., p.s.s.o., rib to last 28 sts., k. 3 tog., rib 25. (4 sts. decreased).
Work 19 rows straight.
Rep. the last 20 rows until 97 (103; 109; 115) sts. remain.
Work straight until front measures same as right half of back up to armhole shaping, ending after a 2nd rib row.
Shape armholes by casting off 5 (5; 5; 5) sts. at

beg. of next 2 rows. Dec. 1 st. at each end of next 3 rows, then on the 2 (3; 4; 5) following alt. rows. 77 (81; 85; 89) sts.
Work straight until front measures same as back to shoulder. Cast off in rib.

RIGHT SLEEVE

Commence with back half of cuff. With No. 11 (3 mm) needles, cast on 25 (27; 29; 31) sts.
Work 31 rows in rib as before.
Next row: Rib to last 9 sts., cast off 9 sts. Break yarn. Slip remaining 16 (18; 20; 22) sts. on a spare needle.
Now work front half of cuff. With No. 11 (3 mm) needles, cast on 35 sts. for all sizes.
1st to 4th rows: In rib as before.
5th row (buttonhole row): Rib 30, cast off 2 sts., rib to end.
6th row: Rib to end casting on 2 sts. where sts. were cast off.
Work 10 rows in rib.
Rep. the last 12 rows once, then 5th and 6th rows again.
Rib 2 more rows.
Next row: Rib to end, then rib across sts. on spare needle.
**Continue on these 51 (53; 55; 57) sts. shaping sleeve by inc. 1 st. at each end of next row, then on every following 12th row until there are 61 (65; 69; 73) sts., taking extra sts. into rib.
Work straight until sleeve measures 28 cm. (11 in.), ending after a wrong-side row.
Change to No. 9 (3¾ mm) needles and beg. k. row work 2 rows in st.st.
Shape sleeve thus:
1st inc. row: K. 3 (5; 7; 9), (m.1, k. 5) to last 3 (5; 7; 9) sts., m.1, k. 3 (5; 7; 9). 73 (77; 81; 85) sts.
Work 9 rows straight.
2nd inc. row: K. 4 (6; 8; 10), (m.1, k. 5, m.1, k. 7) 5 times, m.1, k. 5, m.1, k. 4 (6; 8; 10). 85 (89; 93; 97) sts.
Work 9 rows straight.
3rd inc. row: K. 5 (7; 9; 11), (m.1, k. 5, m.1, k. 9) 5 times, m.1, k. 5, m.1, k. 5 (7; 9; 11). 97 (101; 105; 109) sts.
Work 9 rows straight.
4th inc. row: K. 6 (8; 10; 12), (m.1, k. 5, m.1, k. 11) 5 times, m.1, k. 5, m.1, k. 6 (8; 10; 12). 109 (113; 117; 121) sts.
Work 9 rows straight.
5th inc. row: K. 7 (9; 11; 13), (m.1, k. 5, m.1, k. 13) 5 times, m.1, k. 5, m.1, k. 7 (9; 11; 13). 121 (125; 129; 133) sts.
Work straight until sleeve measures 44 cm. (17½ in.) at centre, ending after a p. row.
Shape top by casting off 6 (7; 8; 9) sts. at beg. of next 2 rows.
Dec. 1 st. at each end of every k. row until 77 sts. remain.
Purl 1 row.
Next row: K. to last 4 sts., turn.
Next row: Sl. 1, p. to last 4 sts., turn.
Next 2 rows: Sl. 1, work to last 8 sts., turn.
Next 2 rows: Sl. 1, work to last 12 sts., turn.
Next 2 rows: Sl. 1, work to last 16 sts., turn.
Next row: Sl. 1, k. to end. Cast off.

LEFT SLEEVE

Commence with front half of cuff. With No. 11 (3 mm) needles, cast on 35 sts. for all sizes.

1st to 4th rows: In rib as before.
5th row (buttonhole row): Rib 3, cast off 2 sts., rib to end.
6th row: In rib casting on 2 sts. in each place where sts. were cast off.
Work 10 rows in rib.
Rep. the last 12 rows once, then 5th and 6th rows again.
Rib 2 more rows. Slip sts. on a spare needle.
Now work back half of cuff. With No. 11 (3 mm) needles, cast on 25 (27; 29; 31) sts.
Work 31 rows in rib as before.
Next row: Cast off 9 sts., rib to end.
Next row: Rib to end, then rib across sts. on spare needle.
Complete as right sleeve working from ** to end.

BORDERS

With No. 11 (3 mm) needles, cast on 9 sts. Work a strip in rib to fit, when slightly stretched, up right back edge to shoulder. Cast-off in rib.
Mark position on border for 9 buttons, 1st to be 5 cm. (2 in.) from lower edge and remainder spaced evenly above up to start of front slope.
Make 2nd strip as first but with holes to match markers thus:
1sr row: Rib 3, cast off 3 sts., rib to end.
2nd row: In rib casting on 3 over those cast off.

TO MAKE UP

Do not press. Join shoulder, side and sleeve seams. Sew in sleeves easing in fullness at top. Sew on borders and buttons.

Robert White

ABSTRACT GEOMETRIC SWEATER

Robert White, the New York tenor adored for his Irish romantic singing on both sides of the Atlantic, is especially adored by the Queen Mother and Prince Charles. The TV star, whose repertoire includes Beethoven and opera, can pull huge audiences at London's Festival Hall.

MATERIALS

Patons Siberia (**M**-2190)	**50 g. balls**	7	7	8	8
Patons Beehive Chunky (**A**-9354)	**50 g. balls**	4	4	4	5
Patons Beehive Chunky (**B**-9340)	**50 g. balls**	4	4	4	4

Pair Milward needles each Nos. 5 (5½ mm) and 7 (4½ mm).

MEASUREMENTS

To fit chest	**cm.**	97	102	107	112
	in.	38	40	42	44
Length from shoulder	**cm.**	65	66	67	69
	in.	25½	26	26½	27
Sleeve seam	**cm.**	52	52	52	52
	in.	20½	20½	20½	20½

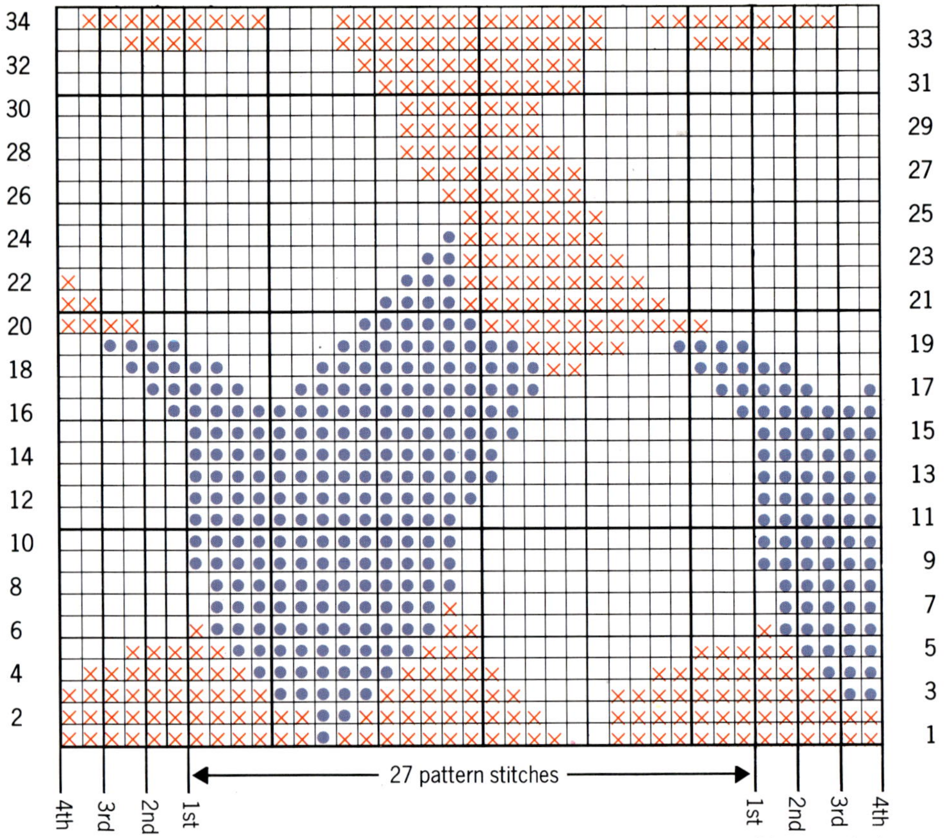

odd sts. worked at beg. of k. rows and end of p. rows for various sizes.

odd sts. worked at end of k. rows and beg. of p. rows for various sizes

KEY
× = A Beehive 9354
● = B Beehive 9340
□ = M Siberia 2190

TENSION

Instructions are based on a standard stocking stitch tension of 15 sts. and 20 rows to 10 cm. (4 in.) using Siberia and No. 5 (5½ mm) needles.

ABBREVIATIONS

k., knit; **p.**, purl; **sts.**, stitches; **patt.**, pattern; **st.st.**, stocking stitch; **inc.**, increase, increasing; **dec.**, decrease, decreasing; **beg.**, beginning; **alt.**, alternate; **rep.**, repeat; **cm.**, centimetres; **in.**, inches.

FRONT

With No. 7 (4½ mm) needles and M, cast on 64 (68; 72; 76) sts.

1st row: (right side): K. 3, (p. 2, k. 2) to last st., k. 1.

2nd row: K. 1, (p. 2, k. 2) to last 3 sts., p. 2, k. 1.

Rep. these 2 rows for 10 cm. (4 in.), ending after a 1st row.

Next row: Rib 2 (4; 6; 8), (inc. in next st., rib 3, inc. in next st., rib 3, inc. in next st., rib 2) 5 times, inc. in next st., rib 3, inc. in next st., rib to end. 81 (85; 89; 93) sts.

Change to No. 5 (5½ mm) needles and patt. thus:–

(**N.B.**: Use a separate ball of yarn for each colour area, twisting yarn on wrong side where necessary when changing colour to avoid a hole).

Work rows 1 to 34 of patt. from chart working in st.st., beg. k. row, repeating the 27 patt. sts. 3 times across and working odd sts., at each end of rows as indicated for the various sizes.

These 34 rows form patt.

Continue in patt. until work measures 57 (57; 58; 58) cm., 22½ (22½; 23; 23) in. from beg., ending after a p. row.

Keeping patt. correct, shape neck thus:–

Next row: Patt. 34 (35; 37; 38), turn. Continue on this group.

Dec. 1 st. at neck edge on next 4 rows. 30 (31; 33; 34) sts.

Work straight until front measures 65 (66; 67; 69) cm., 25½ (26; 26½; 27) in. from beg., ending at side edge.

Shape shoulder by casting off 10 (10; 11; 11) sts. at beg. of next and following alt. row. Work 1 row. Cast off.

With right side facing, slip centre 13 (15; 15; 17) sts. on a spare needle. Rejoin appropriate colour and patt. 1 row. Complete as first half.

BACK
Omitting neck shaping, work as front to shoulder shaping, ending after a p. row.
Shape shoulders by casting off 10 (10; 11; 11) sts. at beg. of next 4 rows, then 10 (11; 11; 12) sts. at beg. of next 2 rows. Slip final 21 (23; 23; 25) sts. on a spare needle.

SLEEVES
With No. 7 (4½ mm) needles, cast on 32 (32; 36; 36) sts.
Work in rib as on welt for 10 cm. (4 in.), ending after a 1st row.
1st and 2nd sizes only:
Next row: Rib 2, (inc. once in each of next 3 sts., rib 1) 7 times, inc. in next st., rib 1.
3rd and 4th sizes only:
Next row: (Inc. in next st., rib 1) 18 times.

All sizes:
Change to No. 5 (5½ mm) needles and work in patt. on these 54 sts. thus:–
Work rows 1 and 2 of patt. from chart working the 27 patt. sts. twice across for all sizes.
Continue in patt. as placed on last 2 rows shaping sides by inc. 1 st. at each end of 5th (9th; 9th; 13th) row following, then on every following 8th (6th; 5th; 4th) row until there are 72 (76; 80; 84) sts., taking extra sts. into patt.
Work straight until sleeve measures 52 cm. (20½ in.) from beg. Cast off in M.

NECKBAND
First join left shoulder. With No. 7 (4½ mm) needles and M, right side facing, k. up 72 (76; 76; 80) sts. evenly round neck, including sts. on spare needles. Beg. 2nd row work 7 rows in rib as on welt. Cast off loosely in rib.

COLLAR
With No. 7 (4½ mm) needles and M, cast on 120 (124; 124; 128) sts.
Work in rib as on welt for 13 cm. (5 in.).
Shape neck edge thus:–
1st and 2nd rows: Rib to last 10 sts., turn.
3rd and 4th rows: Rib to last 20 sts., turn.
5th and 6th rows: Rib to last 30 sts., turn.
7th and 8th rows: Rib to last 40 sts., turn.
9th row: Rib to end. Cast off firmly.

TO MAKE UP
Do not press. Join right shoulder and edges of neckband. Stitch cast-off edges of sleeves in position to yoke, then join side and sleeve seams. Stitch shaped edge of collar to inside of base of neckband.

Audrey Eyton and Zoe Brown

THROW AROUND SHAWLS

Audrey Eyton is elegant and extremely slender by nature – or did the famous '*F-Plan*' diet which she invented and which changed our eating habits help? For her country life Audrey chooses this elegant throw around fringed shawl. Zoe Brown, a mountaineer's daughter and now the teenage voice of BBC's *Breakfast Time*, is Audrey Eyton's niece. She loves her aunt's county-lady shawl and wears a version hotted up with wild stripes.

MATERIALS

Striped Version

Patons Beehive DK

	A (6207)	**50 g. balls**	3
	B (6213)	**50 g. balls**	2
	C (6209)	**50 g. balls**	2

Plain Version

Patons Moorland Tweed DK	**50 g. balls**	7

Pair No. 7 (4½ mm) knitting needles.

MEASUREMENTS

Depth approx.	**cm.**	72
	in.	28

TENSION

19 sts. and 38 rows to 10 cm. (4 in.) measured over garter stitch on No. 7 (4½ mm) needles.

ABBREVIATIONS

k., knit; **g.st.**, garter stitch (every row k.); **dec.**, decrease; **beg.**, beginning; **alt.**, alternate; **rep.**, repeat; **patt.**, pattern; **cont.**, continue; **foll.**, following; **rem.**, remaining; **r.s.**, right side; **cm.**, centimetres; **mm.**, millimetres; **in.**, inches.

STRIPE PATTERN

36 rows A, 36 rows B, 36 rows C and 36 rows D. These 144 rows form stripe patt.

STRIPED VERSION

With No. 7 (4½ mm) needles and A, cast on 280 sts. and k. 1 row.

Work in stripe patt., joining in and breaking off colours as required, at the same time shaping sides by dec. 1 st. at each end of 3rd and every foll. 4th row until 266 sts. rem. Work 1 row.

Now dec. 1 st. at each end of next and every foll. alt. row until 2 sts. rem., ending with r.s. facing.

Cast off rem. sts.

TO FINISH

Do not press.

Cut remaining yarn into 30 cm. (12 in.) lengths and using appropriate colour next to each stripe as in photograph, take 4 strands together each time, knot a fringe along the 2 shaped edges.

Trim fringes.

PLAIN VERSION

Work as for striped version but using only one colour throughout.

Debi Brett

DARING BARE MIDRIFF DRESS

Debi Brett, the top model who was dubbed 'The Most Beautiful Girl In The World', has a stunning 21-inch waist. The rest of her is pretty amazing too and is set off to perfection in this pale grey and peach striped dress for girls with slender waists and a taste for daring summer fashion.

MATERIALS

Patons Cotton Perle, **MS** (Grey)	**50 g. balls**	7	7	8
C (Peach)	**50 g. balls**	3	3	3

Pair needles each Nos.9 (3¾ mm) and 11 (3 mm).

MEASUREMENTS

To fit bust	**cm.**	81	86	91
	in.	32	34	36
Length from shoulder when worn approximately	**cm.**	90	93	96
	in.	35¾	36½	37¾

TENSION

Approximately 12 sts. and 14½ rows to 5 cm. (2 in.) over rib, not stretched, on No. 9 (3¾ mm) needles.

ABBREVIATIONS

k., knit; **p.**, purl; **sts.**, stitches; **g.st.**, garter st.; **patt.**, pattern; **inc.**, increase, increasing; **beg.**, beginning; **alt.**, alternate; **rep.**, repeat; **cm.**, centimetres; **in.**, inches.

LOWER FRONT

With No. 9 (3¾ mm) needles and MS, cast on 95 (101; 107) sts.
Work in patt. thus:–
1st row (right side): In MS, k.
2nd row: In MS, p. 2, (k. 1, p. 1) to last st., p. 1.
3rd row: In MS, k. 2, (p. 1, k. 1) to last st., k. 1.
4th to 10th rows: Rep. 2nd and 3rd rows 3 times, then 2nd row again.
11th to 14th rows: In C, as 1st to 4th.
These 14 rows from patt.
Continue in patt. until work measures 41 cm. (16 in.) at centre, ending after a right-side row.
Work diagonal shaping thus:–
Keeping rib correct, cast off 8 (14; 20) sts. at beg. of next row, then 5 sts. at beg. of every following alt. row until 12 sts. remain. Now cast off 4 sts. at beg. of the 2 following alt. rows.
Work 1 row. Cast off final 4 sts.

LOWER BACK

Work as lower front but ending after a wrong-side row before shaping.

UPPER FRONT

With No. 9 (3¾ mm) needles and MS, cast on 2 sts. and k. 1 row. Continue in striped patt., shaping by inc. 1 st. at beg. of 1st row and at same edge on every row until there are 8 sts. taking extra sts. into rib.
Now cast on 4 sts. at shaped edge on every alt. row until there are 84 (88; 92) sts., finally cast on 7 (9; 11) sts. at beg. of following alt. row. 91 (97; 103) sts. Mark centre of last row.
Work straight until front measures 7 (7; 9) cm., 2¾ (3; 3¾) in. from marker, ending after a wrong-side row.
Shape armholes and one shoulder neckline thus:–
1st row: Cast off 9 (12; 15) sts., work to end
2nd row: Cast off 3 (6; 9) sts., work to end.
3rd row: Work 2 tog., work to end.
4th row: Cast off 3 sts., work to last 2 sts., work 2 tog.
5th to 8th rows: Rep. 3rd and 4th rows twice. 64 sts.
9th row: Work 2 tog., work to end.
10th row: Cast off 3 sts., work to end.
11th to 22nd rows: Rep. 9th and 10th rows 6 times. 36 sts. Now cast off 3 sts. at beg. of every following alt. row until 12 sts. remain. Finally dec. 1 st. at neck edge on every following alt. row until 9 sts. remain.
Work a few rows straight until front measures 19 (20; 21) cm., 7½ (8; 8½) in. from beg. of armhole shaping. Cast off in rib.

UPPER BACK

Work as upper front but working shapings at opposite edges, thus 1st increase at commencement will be at *end* of row.

BORDERS

With No. 11 (3 mm) needles and MS, right side facing, k. up 70 (76; 84) sts. evenly along shaped edge of lower front.
Work 6 rows in g.st. Cast off.
Rep. for lower back.
Work borders similarly for lower edges of upper front and back but knitting up 6 sts. fewer.
With No. 11 (3 mm) needles and MS, right side facing, k. up 69 (75; 81) sts. evenly along upper shaped neck edge of front.
Work 6 rows in g.st. Cast off.
Rep. for back.
Join shoulder. Now finally with No. 11 (3 mm) needles and MS, right side facing, k. up 100 (110; 120) sts. evenly round armhole.
Work 6 rows in g.st. Cast off.

TO MAKE UP

Do not press. Join all side seams and edges of borders. Press seams following pressing instructions. Catch upper and lower sections together at waist.

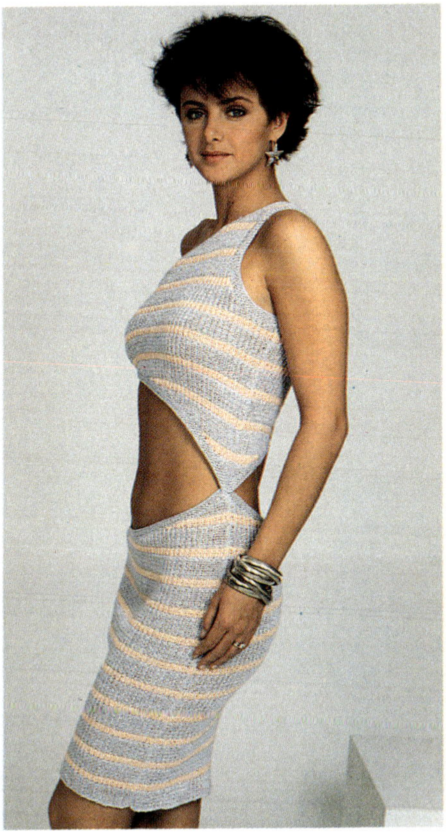

Susannah York

THE BEAUTIFUL BATWING

One of our finest and best loved British actresses, Miss York broke our hearts in the television series *We'll Meet Again*. In private, Susannah, mother of two, favours the quiet pastel shades that traditionally complement an English beauty.

MATERIALS

Patons Linen Look

Caraway (**A**)	**50 g. balls**	6	7	8	9
Oyster (**B**)	**50 g. balls**	2	2	2	2

Pair each Nos. 8 (4 mm), 7 (4½ mm) and 11 (3 mm) knitting needles. Approx. 55 small beads. 1 crochet hook size 3.50 mm

MEASUREMENTS

To fit bust	**cm.**	81	86	91	96
	in.	32	34	36	38
Length from shoulder to hem	**cm.**	54	56	58	60
	in.	21	22	23	24
Sleeve seam approx.	**cm.**	43	44	45	46
	in.	17	17	18	18

TENSION

22 sts. and 30 rows to 10 cm. (4 in.) over st.st. on No. 8 (4 mm) needles.

ABBREVIATIONS

k., knit; **p.**, purl; **cm.**, centimetres; **in.**, inches; **rep.**, repeat; **rem.**, remaining; **foll.**, following; **beg.**, beginning; **alt.**, alternate; **inc.**, increase; **dec.**, decrease; **sts.**, stitches; **patt.**, pattern; **r.s.**, right side; **w.s.**, wrong side; **d.c.**, double crochet; **cont.**, continue.

BACK

**With No. 11 (3 mm) needles and A, cast on 111 (115; 119; 123) sts. and work in rib as follows:

1st row: * K. 1, p. 1, rep. from * to last st., k. 1.

2nd row: * P. 1, k. 1, rep. from * to last st., p. 1.

Rep. these 2 rows to form rib and work straight in rib as set until piece measures 13 cm. (5 in.) from beg. ending w.s. row.

Change to No. 8 (4 mm) needles and st.st. (*1st row:* k., *2nd row:* p.) and work in stripe sequence as follows:

* st.st. 12 rows A, st.st. 2 rows B, rep. from * to end of work.

Work straight in stripes as set until piece measures 21 (23; 25; 27) cm. 8 (9; 10; 10½) in. from beg. ending w.s. row.

Inc. 1 st. at each end of next 5 rows, then cast on 2 sts. at beg. of next 10 rows.

Cast on 3 sts. at beg. of next 12 rows, then cast on 10 sts. at start of next 2 rows.

Cast on 20 sts. at beg. of next 2 rows and 21 (23; 25; 27) sts. at start of foll. 2 rows. 279 (287; 295; 303) sts. on needle. **

Work straight in patt. as set on these sts. until piece measures 51 (53; 55; 57) cm. 20 (21; 21½; 22) in. from beg., ending w.s. row.

Next row: Patt. 125 (128; 131; 134) sts. then leave next 29 (31; 33; 35) sts. on spare pin, then patt. rem. sts.

Now cont. in patt. as set on these last sts. only and work 1 row.

Cast off 3 sts. at beg. of next and every foll. alt. row 4 times in all, then work 1 row.

Cast off rem. 113 (116; 119; 122) sts.

Rejoin yarn to neck edge of rem. sts. and complete to match first side, reversing all shapings.

FRONT

Work as for back from ** to **.

Work straight in patt. as set on these sts. until piece measures 46 (48; 50; 52) cm. 18 (19; 19½; 20) in. from beg. ending w.s. row.

Next row: Patt. 131 (134; 137; 140) sts. then leave next 17 (19; 21; 23) sts. on spare pin, then patt. to end.

Now cont. in patt. as set on these last sts. and work 1 row.

Cast off 5 sts. at beg. of next row, 3 sts. at start of foll. alt. row and 2 sts. at beg. of next alt. row, then work 1 row.

Dec. 1 st. at beg. of next and every foll. alt. row 8 times in all, then work 1 row.

Work straight in patt. on these rem. sts. until front matches back to shoulder, ending same patt. row as for back.

Cast off.

Rejoin yarn to neck edge of rem. sts. and complete to match first side, reversing all shapings.

COLLAR

Join right shoulder seam. With r.s. of work facing, No. 8 (4 mm) needles and A, pick up and k. 21 sts. from side front neck edge, then k. across 17 (19; 21; 23) sts. from pin at centre front, then pick up and k. 21 sts. from rem. front neck edge, then pick up and k. 13 sts. from side back neck edge, then k. across 29 (31; 33; 35) sts. from pin at centre back, then pick up and k. 13 sts. from rem. side back neck edge.

Change to st.st. and stripe patt. as for body, and work straight for 12 cm. (5 in.) starting with k. row and ending with p. row.

Change to No. 7 (4½ mm) needles and work as set until piece measures 23 cm. (9 in.) from beg. ending p. row.

K. 4 rows then cast off.

CUFFS

Join rem. shoulder seam, cont. up collar, and reversing seam for collar.

With r.s. of work facing, No. 11 (3 mm) needles and A, pick up and k. 89 sts. from along sleeve edge.

Next row: P. 1, * p. 2 tog., rep. from * to end. 45 sts.

Change to rib as for welts and work straight until piece measures 6 cm. (2 in.) from beg., ending w.s. row.

Cast of ribwise.

Rep. for other side.

PICOT EDGING

With 3.50 mm crochet hook and w.s. of work facing, work 2 rows of d.c. around edge of collar.

TO MAKE UP

Join side seams. Do not press. Darn in loose ends. Fold collar onto r.s. of work. Sew beads round edge of collar.

Hot Gossip

DANCE AND EXERCISE GEAR

Hot Gossip, the group who put the heat into dancing on television, is also one of Britain's most successful touring groups. Arlene Phillips, international choreographer of the hit stage show *Starlight Express,* is responsible for their extraordinary style and motion. Hot Gossip like to show off their perfectly fit bodies in dance and exercise-based clothes.

GREY AND PINK RUNNER'S DELIGHT

Floid wears a gorgeous grey and pink tracksuit with matching fisherman's rib sweater and nifty pink and grey striped leg-warmers. All machine washable.

SWEATER

MATERIALS

Patons Beehive DK (**MS**)	**50 g. balls**	8	9	10
(**C**)	**50 g. balls**	1	1	2

Pair each No. 10 (3¼ mm) and No. 8 (4 mm) knitting needles.

MEASUREMENTS

To fit chest	**cm.**	91	97	102
	in.	36	38	40
Length	**cm.**	66	67	68
	in.	26	26	27
Sleeve seam	**cm.**	46	46	47
	in.	18	18	18½

TENSION

22 sts. and 30 rows to 10 cm. (4 in.) measured over st.st. on No. 8 (4 mm) needles.

ABBREVIATIONS

k., knit; **p.**, purl; **st.st.**, stocking stitch; **st.**, stitch; **tog.**, together; **inc.**, increase; **dec.**, decrease; **beg.**, beginning; **alt.**, alternate; **rep.**, repeat; **patt.**, pattern; **cont.**, continue; **foll.**, following; **rem.**, remaining; **r.s.**, right side; **w.s.**, wrong side; **cm.**, centimetres; **mm.**, millimetres; **in.**, inches; **m.1**, make 1 stitch by picking up horizontal loop lying before next stitch and working into back of it; **MS.**, Main Shade; **C.**, Contrast.

STRIPE PATTERN

K. 2 rows C., (p. 1 row C., k. 1 row C.) 4 times, (k. 1 row MS., p. 1 row MS.) 5 times.
These 20 rows form stripe patt.

BACK

**With No. 10 (3¼ mm) needles and MS., cast on 100 [106; 112] sts. and work in k. 1, p. 1 rib for 7 cm. (2½ in.).
Next row: Rib 5 [8; 3], m.1, (rib 6 [6; 7], m.1) 15 times, rib 5 [8; 4]. 116 [122; 128] sts.
Change to No. 8 (4 mm) needles and work in st.st. until back measures 40 cm. (15½ in.) ending with r.s. facing.
Shape raglans by casting off 5 [6; 7] sts. at beg. of next 2 rows.
Dec. 1 st. at each end of next row. Work 3 rows.
Rep. last 4 rows 3 [4; 5] times more.**
Now dec. 1 st. at each end of next and every foll. alt. row until 38 [40; 42] sts. rem. ending with r.s. facing.
Leave rem. sts. on a spare needle.

FRONT

Work as for back from ** to **.
Now dec. 1 st. at each end of next and every foll. alt. row until 62 [64; 66] sts. rem., ending with r.s. facing.
Divide for neck, as folls.:
Next row: K. 2 tog., k. 18, k. 2 tog., turn and leave rem. sts. on a spare needle.
Work 1 row.
Dec. 1 st. at raglan and neck edge on next and every alt. row until 6 sts. rem. ending with r.s. facing.
Cont. dec. at raglan only on every alt. row until 2 sts. rem., ending with r.s. facing.
Next row: K. 2 tog. and fasten off.
With r.s. facing, slip centre 18 [20; 22] sts. on a length of yarn, rejoin yarn to rem. sts., k. 2 tog., k. to last 2 sts., k. 2 tog.
Work to match first side, reversing shapings.

SLEEVES

With No. 10 (3¼ mm) needles and MS., cast on 52 [54; 56] sts. and work in k. 1, p. 1 rib for 6 cm. (2 in.).
Next row: Rib 4 [5; 6], m.1, [rib 4, m.1) 11 times, rib 4 [5; 6]. 64 [66; 68] sts.
Change to No. 8 (4 mm) needles and work in st.st. shaping sides by inc. 1 st. at each end of 5th and every foll. 8th row until there are 88 [90; 92] sts.
Work straight until sleeve measures 46 [46; 47] cm. 18 (18; 18½) in. ending with r.s. facing.
Work in stripe patt., shape raglans by casting off 5 [6; 7] sts. at beg. of next 2 rows.
Dec. 1 st. at each end of next row. Work 3 rows.
Rep. last 4 rows 5 [7; 9] times more. 66 [62; 58] sts.
Now dec. 1 st. at each end of next and every foll. alt. row until 14 sts. rem., ending with r.s. facing.
Leave rem. sts. on a spare needle.

MAKE UP AND NECK BORDER

Do not press.
Join raglans, leaving left back raglan open.
Neck border
With r.s. facing, No. 10 (3¼ mm) needles and MS, k. 14 sts. from sleeve dec. 2 sts. evenly, knit up 22 sts. down left side of neck, k. 18 [20; 22] sts. from front, knit up 22 sts. up right side of neck, k. 14 sts. from sleeve dec. 2 sts evenly, k. 38 [40; 42] sts. from back. 124 [128; 132] sts.
Work in k. 1, p. 1 rib for 7 cm. (2½ in.).
Using a No. 8 (4 mm) needle, cast off loosely in rib.
Join rem. raglan and neck border.
Fold neck border in half to w.s. and slip hem loosely in position. Join side and sleeve seams.

TRACKSUIT TROUSERS

MATERIALS

Patons Beehive DK (**MS**)	**50 g. balls**	8	8	9
(**C**)	**50 g. balls**	1	1	2

Pair each No. 10 (3¼ mm) and No. 8 (4 mm) knitting needles.

MEASUREMENTS

To fit hips	**cm.**	92	98	103
	in.	36	38½	40½
Inside leg seam (adjustable)	**cm.**	81	82	83
	in.	32	32	32½

TENSION
22 sts. and 30 rows to 10 cm. (4 in.) measured over st.st. on No. 8 (4 mm) needles.

ABBREVIATIONS
k., knit; **p.**, purl; **st.**, stitch; **st.st.**, stocking stitch; **sl.1k.**, slip one knitways; **sl.1p.**, slip one purlways; **tog.**, together; **inc.**, increase; **dec.**, decrease; **beg.**, beginning; **alt.**, alternate; **rep.**, repeat; **patt.**, pattern; **cont.**, continue; **foll.**, following, **rem.**, remaining; **r.s.**, right side; **w.s.**, wrong side; **cm.**, centimetres; **mm.**, millimetres; **in.**, inches; **MS.**, Main Shade; **C.**, Contrast; **rev.**, reverse; **m.1**, make 1 stitch by picking up horizontal loop lying before next stitch and working into back of it.

STRIPE PATT.
K. 2 rows in C. (p. 1 row in C., k. 1 row in C.) 4 times, (k. 1 row in MS., p. 1 row in MS.) 5 times. These 20 rows form stripe and rev.st.st. patt.

RIGHT LEG
**With No. 10 (3¼ mm) needles and MS., cast on 48 [50; 52] sts. and work in k. 1, p. 1 rib for 12 cm. (4 ½ in.).
Next row: (Rib 1, m.1) 46 [48; 50] times, rib 2. 94 [98; 102] sts.
Change to No. 8 (4 mm) needles and work in st.st. shaping sides by inc. 1 st. at each end of 3rd and every foll. 8th row until work measures 36 [37; 38] cm. 14 (14½; 15) in., ending with r.s. facing.
Work 50 rows in stripe patt. as given *at the same time* shaping sides as before, then work in st.st. still shaping sides until there are 134 [140; 146] sts.
Work straight until leg measures 81 [82; 83] cm., 32 (32; 32½) in., ending with r.s. facing.
Shape crotch by casting off 5 sts. at beg. of next 2 rows until 108 [114; 120] sts. rem.
Work straight until leg measures 22 cm. (8½ in.) from beg. of crotch shaping, ending with r.s. facing.**
Shape as folls:
1st row: K.
2nd row: P. 54 [57; 60], turn.
3rd row: S1.1k., k. to end.
4th row: P. 41 [43; 45], turn.
5th row: As 3rd.
6th row: P. 28 [29; 30], turn.
7th row: As 3rd.
8th row: P. 15, turn.
9th row: As 3rd.
10th row: P. across all sts.
***Change to No. 10 (3¼ mm) needles and work
Next row: K. 3 [6; 9], k. 2 tog., (k. 2, k. 2 tog.) 25 times, k. 3 [6; 9]. 82 [88; 94] sts.
Work in k. 1, p. 1 rib until waist ribbing measures 15 cm. (6 in.) ending with r.s. facing.
Cast off.

LEFT LEG
Work as for right leg from ** to **.
Shape as folls.:
1st row: K. 54 [57; 60], turn.
2nd row: S1.1p., p. to end.
3rd row: K. 41 [43; 45], turn.
4th row: As 2nd.
5th row: K. 28 [29; 30], turn.
6th row: As 2nd.
7th row: K. 15, turn.
8th row: As 2nd.
9th row: K. across all sts.
10th rows: P. 1 row.
Cont. as for right leg from *** to end.

BELT CARRIERS (Make 4)
With No. 10 (3¼ mm) needles and MS., cast on 7 sts. and work as folls.:
1st row: K. 2, (p. 1, k. 1) twice, k. 1.
2nd row: K. 1, (p. 1, k. 1) 3 times.
Rep. these 2 rows for 4 cm. (1½ in.).
Cast off.

MAKE UP
Do not press.
Join front and back crotch seams, then inside leg seams.
Position belt carriers 2 cm. (½ in.) above start of waist ribbing and even around waistline.

FISHERMAN'S RIB SWEATER

MATERIALS

Patons Beehive DK	**50 g. balls**	10	11	12

Pair each No. 10 (3¼ mm) and No. 8 (4 mm) knitting needles.

MEASUREMENTS

To fit chest	**cm.**	91	97	102
	in.	36	38	40
Length	**cm.**	66	67	68
	in.	26	26	27
Sleeve seam	**cm.**	46	46	47
	in.	18	18	18½

TENSION

22 sts. and 30 rows to 10 cm. (4 in.) measured over stocking stitch on No. 8 (4 mm) needles.
20 sts. and 40 rows to 10 cm. (4 in.) measured over rib pattern on No. 8 (4 mm) needles.

ABBREVIATIONS

k., knit; **p.**, purl; **st.**, stitch; **tog.**, together; **inc.**, increase; **dec.**, decrease; **beg.**, beginning; **alt.**, alternate; **rep.**, repeat; **patt.**, pattern; **cont.**, continue; **foll.**, following; **rem.**, remaining; **r.s.**, right side; **w.s.**, wrong side; **cm.**, centimetres; **mm.**, millimetres; **in.**, inches; **k.1blw.**, k. 1 below, knit into next stitch one row below, at the same time slipping off stitch above.

BACK

**With No. 10 (3¼ mm) needles, cast on 105 (111; 117) sts., and work in rib as folls.:
1st row: (R.S.), k. 1, *p. 1, k. 1; rep. from * to end.
2nd row: P. 1, *k. 1, p. 1; rep. from * to end.
Rep. these 2 rows until rib measures 7 cm. (2½ in.) ending with r.s. facing.
Change to No. 8 (4 mm) needles and work in fisherman's rib patt. as folls.:
1st row: (r.s.), k. 1, *p. 1, k.1blw.; rep. from * to last 2 sts, p. 1, k. 1.
2nd row: K.
These 2 rows form patt.
Cont. in patt. until back measures 40 cm. (16 in.), ending with r.s. facing.
Shape raglans, keeping continuity of patt., by casting off 5 sts. at beg. of next 2 rows.**
Dec. 1 st. at each end of next and every foll. 4th row until 53 (59; 65) sts. rem.
Work 3 rows.
Now dec. 1 st. at each end of next and every alt. row until 35 (37; 39) sts. rem., ending with r.s. facing.
Leave rem. sts. on a spare needle.

FRONT

Work as for back from ** to **.
Dec. 1 st. at each end of next and every foll. 4th row until 59 (63; 67) sts. rem.
Work 1 row.
Divide for neck, keeping continuity of patt., as folls.:
Next row: Patt. 21 (22; 23) sts., k. 2 tog., turn and leave rem. sts. on a spare needle.
Cont. on these sts. for first side as folls.:
Work 1 row.
Dec. 1 st. at raglan edge on every 4th row as before at the same time dec. 1 st. at neck edge on every alt. row until 11 (15; 19) sts. rem.
Work 1 row.
Now dec. 1 st. at raglan edge on every alt. row at the same time dec. at neck edge on every alt. row as before until 9 sts. rem.
Work 1 row.
Cont dec. at raglan edge only on every alt. row as before until 2 sts. rem., ending with r.s. facing.
Next row: K. 2 tog. and fasten off.
With r.s. facing, slip centre 13 (15; 17) sts. on a length of yarn, rejoin yarn to rem. sts., k. 2 tog., patt. to end.
Work to match first side, reversing shapings.

SLEEVES

With No. 10 (3¼ mm) needles, cast on 53 (55; 57) sts. and work in rib as on back for 8 cm. (3 in.) ending with r.s. facing.
Change to No. 8 (4 mm) needles and work in patt. as on back, shaping sides by inc. 1 st. at each end of 7th and every foll. 10th row until there are 77 (79; 81) sts., taking inc. sts. into patt.
Work straight until sleeve measures 46 (46; 47) cm. 18 (18; 18½) in., ending with r.s. facing.
Shape raglans, keeping continuity of patt., by casting off 5 sts. at beg. of next 2 rows.
Dec. 1 st. at each end of next and every foll. 4th row until 21 sts. rem.
Work 3 rows.
Now dec. 1 st. at each end of next and every alt. row until 11 sts. rem., ending with r.s. facing.
Leave rem. sts. on a spare needle.

MAKE UP AND NECK BORDER

Do not press.
Join raglans, leaving left back raglan open.

NECK BORDER

With No. 10 (3¼ mm) needles, r.s. facing, starting at left sleeve, patt. 11 sts. from left sleeve, knit up 18 sts. down left side of neck, patt. 13 (15; 17) sts. from front, knit up 18 sts. up right side of neck, patt. 11 sts. from right sleeve, patt. 35 (37; 39) sts. from back. 106 (110; 114) sts.
Work in k. 1, p. 1 rib for 7 cm. (2 ½ in.)
Using a No. 8 (4 mm) needle, cast off loosely in rib.
Join left back raglan and neck border.
Fold neck border in half to w.s. and slip hem loosely in position.
Join side and sleeve seams.

PINK NOTHINGS

Frances Wingate makes baby pink look positively adult with these high cut dancer's knickers, delicious wrap-over cardigan, matching wristwarmers and ankle warmers, topped by a headband to keep flying hair in place. All machine washable.

MATERIALS				
Cross-Over Ballet Top				
Patons Beehive	**50 g. balls**	5	5	5
Ballet Knickers				
Patons Beehive DK	**50 g. balls**	2	3	3
Ankle Warmers				
Patons Beehive DK	**50 g. balls**	2	2	2
Wristwarmers				
Patons Beehive DK	**50 g. balls**	1	1	1
Headband				
Patons Beehive DK	**50 g. balls**	1	1	1
Pair each No. 8 (4 mm), No. 10 (3¼ mm) and No. 12 (2¾ mm) needles.				
MEASUREMENTS				
Cross-Over Ballet Top				
To fit bust	**cm.**	81	86	91
	in.	32	34	36
Length from top of shoulders	**cm.**	43	44	44
	in.	17	17½	17½
Sleeve seam	**cm.**	43	43	43
	in.	17	17	17
Ballet knickers	**cm.**	86	91	97
To fit hips	**in.**	34	36	38
Ankle Warmers	**cm.**	28	28	28
Length	**in.**	11	11	11
Wristwarmers				
To fit average wrist				
Headband				
To fit average head				

TENSION

22 sts. and 30 rows measured over 10 cm.(4 in.) of st.st. on No. 8 (4 mm) needles in Double Knitting.

28 sts. and 36 rows measured over 10 cm. (4 in.) of st.st. in Beehive 4-ply on No. 10 (3¼ mm) needles.

ABBREVIATIONS

k., knit; **p.**, purl; **st.**, stitch; **st.st.**, stocking stitch; **g.st.**, garter stitch; **r.s.**, right side; **mm.**, millimetres; **cm.**, centimetres; **in.**, inches; **rep.**, repeat; **dec.**, decrease by working 2 sts. together; **inc.**, increase by working into front and back of st.; **m.1**, pick up horizontal loop lying before next st. and work into back of it; **sl.**, slip; **p.s.s.o.**, pass the slipped st. over; **beg.**, beginning; **tog.**, together; **t.b.l.**, through back of loops; **D.K.**, Beehive D.K.; **4-ply**, Beehive 4-ply.

CROSS-OVER BALLET TOP

Fronts

Left: **With No. 12 (2¾ mm) needles and 4-ply, cast on 99 (105; 113) sts.

1st row: R.s. facing, k. 1, *p. 1, k. 1; rep. from * to end.

2nd row: P. 1, *k. 1, p. 1; rep. from * to end.

Rep. last 2 rows until work measures 4 cm. (1½ in.) ending with 1st row.**

Next row: Cast off 14 sts. in rib, *rib 6 (6; 7), m.1; rep. from *to last 7 (7; 8) sts., rib 7 (7; 8). 98 (105; 112) sts.

Change to No. 10 (3¼ mm) needles.

1st row: R.s facing, knit.

2nd row: K. 7, p. to end.

Keeping 7 sts. at front edge in g.st., continue in st.st., shaping as follows:

Next row: K. to last 9 sts., k. 2 tog., k. 7.

Next row: K. 7 p. to end.

Rep. last 2 rows until 58 (65; 72) sts. remain, ending with r.s. facing.

Continue shaping front edge and at the same time shape armhole as follows:

Next row: Cast off 4, k. to last 9 sts., k. 2 tog. k. 7.

Next row: K. 7, p. to end.

Now dec. 1 st. at armhole edge on next and every alternate row and at the same time continue dec. at front edge on every alternate row as before until 43 (46; 49) sts. remain.

Now keep armhole edge straight and continue dec. at front edge on every alternate row as before until 38 (39; 40) sts. remain, then on every foll. 4th row until 35 (36; 37) sts. remain.

Work straight until front measures 18 (19; 19) cm. 7 (7½; 7½) in. from start of armhole shaping, ending with r.s. facing.

Shape shoulder by casting off 10 (9; 10) sts. at beg. of next row, then 9 (10; 10) sts. at beg. of following 2 alternate rows. Leave remaining 7 sts. on a safety-pin for back neck border.

Right: Work as for left front from ** to **.

Next row: Rib 7 (7; 8), m.1, *rib 6 (6; 7), m.1; rep. from *to last 20 (20; 21) sts., rib 6 (6; 7), cast off remaining 14 sts. in rib.

Rejoin yarn and change to No. 10 (3¼ mm) needles.

1st row: R.s. facing, k.

2nd row: P. to last 7 sts., k. 7.

Finish to correspond with left front, reversing all shapings and noting that 'sl.1, k. 1, p.s.s.o.' will be worked when shaping front edge.

Back

With No. 12 (2¾ mm) needles and 4-ply, cast on 99 (105; 113) sts. and work.

K. 4 cm. (1½ in.) k. 1, p. 1 rib, as for front, ending with 1st row.

Next row: Rib 7, m.1, *rib 6 (6; 7), m.1; rep. from *to last 8 sts., rib 8. 114 (121; 128) sts.

Change to No. 10 (3¼ mm) needles and st.st., starting with a k. row, and work straight until back matches front at side edge, ending with r.s. facing.

Shape armholes by casting off 4 sts. at beg. of next 2 rows, then dec. 1 st. at each end of next and every alternate row until 96 (99; 102) sts. remain.

Work straight until back matches front at armhole edge, ending with r.s. facing.

Shape shoulders by casting off 10 (9; 10) sts. at beg. of next 2 rows, then 9 (10; 10) sts. at beg. of next 4 rows. Cast off remaining sts.

Sleeves

With No. 12 (2¾ mm) needles and 4-ply, cast on 53 (57; 57) sts. and work 4 cm. (1½ in.) k. 1, p. 1 rib as for front, ending with 1st row.

Next row: Rib 4 (6; 6), m.1, *rib 5, m.1; rep. from *to last 4 (6; 6) sts., rib 4 (6; 6). 63 (67; 67) sts.

Change to No. 10 (3¼ mm) needles and st.st., starting with a k. row, shaping sides by inc. 1 st.

at each end of 7th and every following 10th row until there are 87 (91; 91) sts.
Work straight until sleeve seam measures 43 cm. (17 in.), ending with a p. row.
Shape top by casting off 4 sts. at beg. of next 2 rows, then dec. 1 st. at each end of next and every alternate row until 57 sts. remain, all sizes.
P. back, then dec. 1 st. at each end of every row until 21 sts. remain. Cast off.

Neck Border
With No. 12 (2¾ mm) needles and 4-ply, k. across 7 front border sts. on left front and work straight in g.st. until strip fits to centre back of neck. Cast off and work right border to correspond.

Ties
With No. 10 (3¼ mm) needles and 4-ply, cast on 11 sts. and work straight in st.st. until strip measures 56 cm. (22 in.), or length required, ending with r.s. facing.
Next row: K. 11 tog. Fasten off and make another one the same.

BALLET KNICKERS
Back
**With No. 8 (4 mm) needles and D.K., cast on 80 (86; 92) sts.
1st row: K. 1, *k. 1, with yarn at front sl.1; rep. from *to last st., k. 1.
Rep. last row until work measures 18 cm. (7 in.) at centre from start, making sure that an even number of rows has been worked.
Change to st.st., starting with a k. row, and work 16 rows straight.
Shape as follows:
Next row: K. 1, k. 2 tog., k. to last 3 sts., k. 2 tog. t.b.l., k. 1.
Next row: Purl. Rep. last 2 rows until 46 (50; 54) sts. remain.
Next row: P.
Next row: K. 1, k. 3 tog., k. to last 4 sts., k. 3 tog. t.b.l., k. 1.
Next row: P. Rep. last 2 rows until 6 sts. remain, ending with a p. row.**
Cast off.

Front
Work as for back from ** to **.
Work a further 16 rows straight. Cast off.

Ties
With No. 8 (4 mm) needles and D.K., cast on 8 sts. and work 56 cm. (22 in.) st.st., ending with a p. row.
Next row: K. 8 tog. Fasten off and make another one the same.

ANKLE WARMERS
With No. 10 (3¼ mm) needles and D.K., cast on 66 sts.
1st row: R.s. facing, k. 2, *p. 2, k. 2; rep. from * to end.
2nd row: P. 2, *k. 2, p. 2; rep. from * to end.
Rep. last 2 rows until work measures 4 cm. (1½ in.), then change to No. 8 (4 mm) needles and continue in rib until work measures 24 cm. (9½ in.) at centre from start.
Change to No. 10 (3¼ mm) needles and continue until work measures 28 cm. (11 in.) at centre from start. Cast off loosely in rib.

WRIST WARMERS (Make 2)
With No. 8 (4 mm) needles cast on 50 sts. and work in rib as follows:
1st row: K. 2, *p. 2, k. 2; rep. from * to end.
2nd row: P. 2, *k. 2, p. 2; rep. from * to end.
Continue for 12 cm. (5 in.).
Cast off.

HEADBAND
With No. 8 (4 mm) needles cast on 12 sts. and work in st.st. for 64 cm. (25 in.).
Cast off.
Work a second piece the same.

TO MAKE UP
Do not press.
Cross-Over Ballet Top: Join side and sleeve seams; insert sleeves.
Join short ends of back neck border, then pin border in position round neck; sew in position.
Pin cast-on edge of each tie to front edge of ribbing on each front; sew in position.
Ballet Knickers: Join side seams, then join cast-off sts. of crotch together.
Pin cast-on edge of each tie to side seam at end of ribbing; Sew in position.
Ankle Warmers: Join side seam.
Wristwarmers: Do not press. Join seam.
Headband: Twist pieces together to form headband as in photograph.

HANDS ON SHORTS SUIT AND ACCESSORIES

Amanda Abbs sports a trompe l'oeil effect that will be a summer stunner for any extrovert girl. The square cut cropped top teams neatly with roll-bottomed shorts. Both top and bottom boast the hand motif.

MATERIALS				
Shortie Top				
Patons Beehive Double Knitting **(MS)**	**50 g. balls**	4	4	5
(C)	**50 g. balls**	1	1	1
Shorts				
Patons Beehive Double Knitting **(MS)**	**50 g. balls**	5	5	5
(C)	**50 g. balls**	1	1	1
Leg Warmers				
Patons Beehive Double Knitting **(MS)**	**50 g. balls**	5	5	5

Pair each No. 8 (4 mm), No. 10 (3¼ mm) and No. 12 (2¾ mm) needles.
2 buttons for shorts.

MEASUREMENTS				
Shortie Top				
To fit bust	**cm.**	81	86	91
	in.	32	34	36
Length from top of shoulders	**cm.**	39	39	41
	in.	15½	15½	16
Sleeve seam all sizes	**cm.**	18		
	in.	7		
Shorts				
To fit hips	**cm.**	86	91	97
	in.	34	36	38
Length of centre front seam all sizes	**cm.**	44		
	in.	17½		
Leg Warmers				
Length	**cm.**	71		
	in.	28		

TENSION
22 sts. and 30 rows measured over 10 cm. (4 in.) of st.st. on No. 8 (4 mm) needles.

ABBREVIATIONS
k., knit; **p.**, purl; **st.**, stitch; **st.st.**, stocking stitch; **mm.**, millimetres; **cm.**, centimetres; **in.**, inches; **rep.**, repeat; **beg.**, beginning; **sl.**, slip; **inc.**, increase by working into front and back of st.; **tog.**, together; **dec.**, decrease by working 2 sts. together; **r.s.**, right side; **M.**, Main Shade; **C.**, Contrast.

SHORTIE TOP

Back

With No. 12 (2¾ mm) needles, and M. cast on 94 (100; 106) sts. and work 10 rows st.st., starting with a k. row.

Change to No. 8 (4 mm) needles, continue in st.st. and work straight until back measures 18 cm. (7 in.) from start, noting that when taking measurements border must be allowed to roll.

Shape sleeves by casting on 36 sts. at beg. of next 2 rows. 166 (172; 178) sts.

Continue in st.st. until back measures 39 (39; 41) cm. 15½ (15½; 16 in.) from start, ending with r.s. facing.

Shape shoulder by casting off 61 (63; 65) sts. at beg. of next 2 rows. Leave remaining 44 (46; 48) sts. on a spare needle.

Front

Work as for back from ** to **.

Change to No. 8 (4 mm) needles, continue in st.st. and work a further 10 rows straight.

Join in C., starting with 1st row, work hand motifs from chart, reading odd rows knit from right to left and even rows p. from left to right.

Note Twist yarns on wrong side of work when changing colour to avoid a hole, joining in and breaking off yarns as required.

Work straight until front matches back at side edge, ending with r.s. facing.

Continue working motifs and at same time shape sleeves by casting on 36 sts. at beg. of next 2 rows. 166 (172; 178) sts.

Taking extra 36 sts. at each end into st.st. in M., continue working motifs from chart until the 65 rows are done, then break C.

Work straight in st.st. in M. until front measures 32 (32; 33) cm. 12½ (12½; 13) in. at centre from start, ending with r.s. facing.

Here divide for neck.

Next row: K. 72 (74; 76), turn and leave remaining sts. on a spare needle.

Continue on these 72 (74; 76) sts. for first side, dec. 1 st. at neck edge on every row until 61 (63; 65) sts. remain.

Work straight until front matches back at sleeve edge, ending with r.s. facing, then cast off.

With r.s. facing, sl. centre 22 (24; 26) sts. on a spare needle, rejoin yarn to remaining sts., k. to end. Finish to correspond with first side.

Neck Border

Join right shoulder seam.

With r.s. facing, No. 12 (2¾ mm) needles and M., start at left shoulder on front and pick up and k. 22 sts. down left side of neck, k. 22 (24; 26) from centre, pick up and k. 22 up right side, then

k. 44 (46; 48) from back: 110 (114; 118) sts.
***Work 9 rows st.st., starting with a p. row.
Cast off knitways.***

Sleeve Borders
Join left shoulder seam and neck border.
With r.s. facing, No. 12 (2¾ mm) needles and M., pick up and k. 94 (94; 100) sts. along each sleeve edge and work rolled border as for neck border from *** to ***.

SHORTS
Right Leg
**With No. 8 (4 mm) needles and M., cast on 148 (154; 160) sts. and starting with a k. row, work straight in st.st. until work measures 10 cm. (4 in.) at centre from start, ending with a p. row.
Introduce hand motif by turning chart upside down and using left hand of chart as follows:
K. 80 (83; 86) M., work 65th row of chart over next 45 (48; 51) sts., then k. 23.
Next row: P. 23, work 64th row of chart over next 45 (48; 51) sts., then p. 80 (83; 86) M.
Continue thus working hand motif from chart and work a further 6 rows straight.
Continue working hand motif from chart and at the same time shape leg by casting off 3 sts. at beg. of next 2 rows, then dec. 1 st. at each end of next and every alternate row until 116 (122; 128) sts. remain.
Continue working hand motif until the 65 rows are completed, then break C.
Work straight in st.st. in M. until work measures 41 cm. (16 in.) at centre from start, ending with a k. row.**
Shape back as follows:
****1st row:* P. 50 (53; 56), turn.
2nd and every alternate row: Sl. 1, k. to end.
3rd row: P. 36 (39; 42), turn.
5th row: P. 22 (25; 28), turn.
7th row: P. 8 (11; 14), turn.
9th row: P. across all sts., picking up a loop at each point where work was turned and working it together with next st. through back of loops to avoid a hole.
Next row: K. 0 (3; 6), k. 2 tog., *k. 1, k. 2 tog.; rep. from * to last 0 (3; 6) sts., k. 0 (3; 6): 77 (83; 89) sts.***
Change to No. 10 (3¼ mm) needles.
Next row: P. 1, *k. 1, p. 1; rep. from * to end.
Next row: K. 1, *p. 1, k. 1; rep. from * to end.
Rep. last 2 rows until work measures 56 cm. (22 in.) at centre from start. Cast off evenly in rib.

Left Leg
Work as for right leg from ** to **, working 1 row less and omitting hand motif then work from *** to ***, reading 'k.' for 'p.' and 'p.' for 'k.' throughout. Work 1 row. Change to No. 10 (3¼ mm) needles and finish to correspond with right leg.

Side Strips
With No. 10 (3¼ mm) needles and M., cast on 9 sts. 1st row: r.s. facing, k. 2, * p. 1, k. 1; rep. from * to last st., k. 1.
2nd row: K. 1, * p. 1, k. 1;

rep. from * to end.
Rep. last 2 rows until strip measures 13 cm. (5 in.), ending with 2nd row. Make a buttonhole in next 2 rows as follows:
Rib 3, cast off 3, rib to end and back, casting on 3 over those cast off.
Work a further 4 rows k. 1, p. 1 rib. Cast off evenly in rib and make another one the same.

LEG WARMERS
Left Leg
1st piece: With No. 10 (3¼ mm) needles and M., cast on 9 sts. and work 7 cm. (3 in.) k. 1, p. 1 rib as for side strips on shorts, ending with 1st row. **Shape stirrups by inc. 1 st. at each end of next and every alternate row until there are 21 sts., taking inc. sts. into rib. Work 1 row straight.**
2nd piece: Cast on 9 sts. and work 1st and 2nd rows of rib as for 1st piece, then work as for 1st piece from ** to **.
Join pieces together as follows:
Cast on 6 sts., (k. 1, p. 1) 3 times, work in rib across 21 sts. of 1st piece, cast on 11 sts., p. 1, (k. 1, p. 1) 5 times, work in rib across 21 sts. of 2nd piece, cast on 6 sts., (p. 1, k. 1) 3 times: 65 sts.
Continue in k. 1, p. 1 rib until work measures 18 cm. (7 in.) from last set of cast-on sts.
Change to No. 8 (4 mm) needles and st.st., starting with a k. row, and work straight until work measures 53 cm. (21 in.) at centre from cast-on sts., ending with a p. row.
Change to k. 1, p. 1 rib and continue in rib until work measures 71 cm. (28 in.) from last set of cast-on sts., cast off loosely in rib.

Right Leg
Work 1st and 2nd pieces as for left leg, then join pieces together as follows:

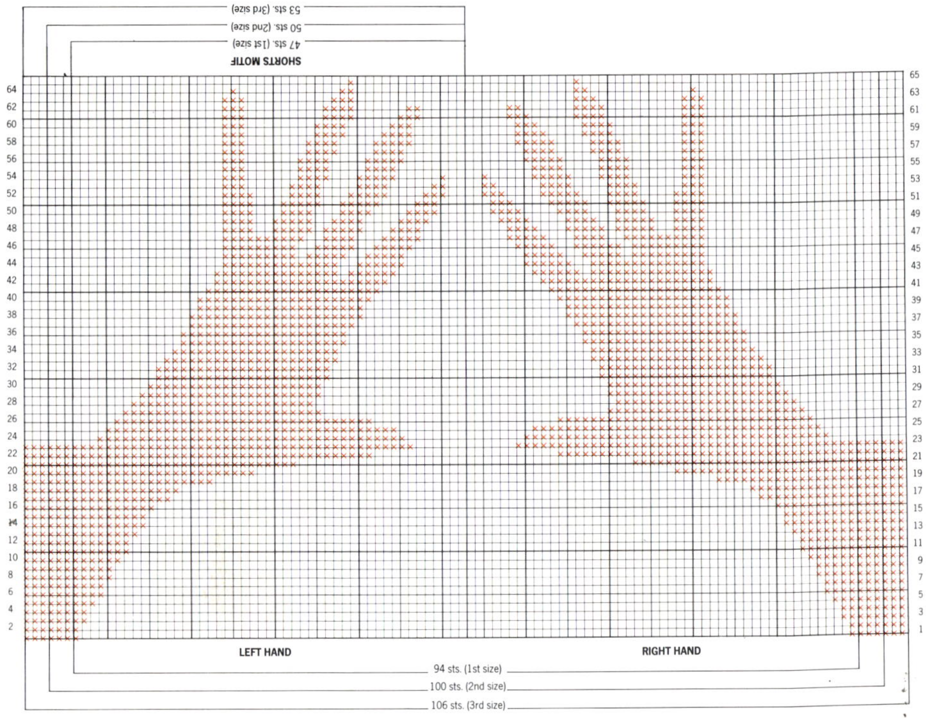

Cast on 6 sts., (k. 1, p. 1) 3 times, rib across 21 sts. of 2nd piece, cast on 11 sts., p. 1 (k. 1, p.1) 5 times, rib across 21 sts. of 1st piece, cast on 6 sts., (p. 1, k. 1) 3 times.
Finish to correspond with left leg.

TO MAKE UP
Shortie Top: Join side and underarm sleeve seams. Press all seams.
Shorts: Join front, back and leg seams. Sew button in centre of each leg, 19 cm. (7½ in.) from cast-on edge.
Sew cast-on edge of side strip on wrong side of work at back of button.
Roll legs and button strip as illustrated.
Leg Warmers: Join cast-on deges of stirrup, then join centre back seam.

TWENTIES PLAYSUIT WITH TOUCH OF SPARKLE

Alison Hierlihy, former Hot Gossip dancer, wears a delicate pink and grey twenties-style playsuit with silver laces at the front and a charming plain headband.

MATERIALS

Patons Cotton Perle **(MS)**	**50 g. balls**	6	7	8
(C)	**50 g. balls**	3	3	3

Pair each No. 11 (3 mm) and No. 8 (4 mm) knitting needles.
Length of silver cord for lacing.
2 buttons.

MEASUREMENTS

To fit bust	**cm.**	81	86	91
	in.	32	34	36

TENSION
22 sts. and 29 rows to 10 cm. (4 in.) measured over st.st. on No. 8 (4 mm) needles.

ABBREVIATIONS
k., knit; **p.**, purl; **st.**, stitch; **st.st.**, stocking stitch; **sl.1k.**, slip 1 knitways; **sl.1p.**, slip 1 purlways; **tog.**, together; **inc.**, increase; **dec.**, decrease; **beg.**, beginning; **alt.**, alternate; **rep.**, repeat; **patt.**, pattern; **cont.**, continue; **foll.**, following; **rem.**, remaining; **r.s.**, right side; **w.s.**, wrong side; **cm.**, centimetres; **mm.**, millimetres; **in.**, inches; **MS.**, Main Shade; **C.**, Contrast; **m.1k.**, make 1 knitways by picking up loop that lies between st.

just worked and following st. and knitting into back of it;
m.1p., make 1 purlways by picking up loop that lies between st. just worked and following st. and purling into back of it.

STRIPE PATT.
10 rows MS., 10 rows C.
These 20 rows form stripe patt.

RIGHT LEG
**With No. 8 (4 mm) needles and MS., cast on 162 (168; 174) sts. and work in st.st. and stripe patt. until work measures 15 cm. (6 in.) ending with r.s. facing.
Shape crotch by casting off 4 sts. at beg. of next 2 rows, then dec. 1 st. at each end of next 5 rows, then on every alt. row until 130 (136; 142) sts. rem.
Work straight until leg measures 24 (25; 26) cm. 9½ (10; 10) in. from start of crotch shaping, ending with r.s. facing.
Break C. and cont. in MS.**
Shape back as folls.:
1st row: K.
2nd row: P. 65 (68; 71), turn.
3rd row: Sl.1k., k. to end.
4th row: P. 32 (34; 36), turn.
5th row: Sl.1k, k. to end.
6th row: P. across all sets.
***Change to No. 11 (3 mm) needles and work as folls.:
Next row: (K. 1, k. 2 tog.) 2 [5; 8] times, (k. 2 tog.) 60 [54; 48] times, (k. 1, k. 2 tog.) 1 [4; 7] times, k. 1. 67 (73; 79) sts.
Next row: P. 1, *k. 1, p. 1; rep. from * to end.
Cont. in k. 1, p. 1 rib as set for 12 more rows.
Change to No. 8 (4 mm) needles:
Mark centre st. (this is for side shaping)
Shape sides as folls.:
1st and 3rd sizes
1st row: Rib to centre st., m.1 k., p. 1, m.1k., rib to end as set.
2nd row: Rib as set.
3rd row: Rib as set to centre st., m.1 p., p. 1, m.1 p., rib as set to end.
4th row: Rib as set.
Rep. last 4 rows 4 times more.
2nd size
1st row: Rib to centre st., m.1p., k. 1, m.1 p., rib to end as set.
2nd row: Rib as set.
3rd row: Rib as set to centre st., m.1 k., k. 1, m.1 k., rib as set to end.
4th row: Rib as set.
Rep. last 4 rows 4 times more.
All sizes
87 (93; 99) sts.
Cont. in k. 1, p. 1 rib until Bodice section measures 29 cm. (11 in.), from beg. of ribbing, ending with w.s. facing.***
Next row: Cast off 44 (48; 50) sts., rib to end.
****Shape as folls.:
Dec. 1 st. at each end of next 8 (8; 6) rows.
3rd Size Only
Cast off 3 sts. at beg. of next 2 rows.
All Sizes
Cast off 3 (3; 4) sts. at beg. of next 2 rows, 4 sts. at beg of foll. 2 rows, then 4 (5; 5) sts. at beg. of next 2 rows. 5 sts. rem.
Cont. in rib as set on these 5 sts., for strap, until strap measures approx. 36 cm. (14 in.), ending with r.s. facing. Cast off rem. sts.

LEFT LEG
Work as for right leg from ** to **.
Shape back as folls.:
1st row: K. 65 (68; 71), turn.
2nd row: Sl.1p., p. to end.
3rd row: K. 32 (34; 36), turn.
4th row: Sl.1p., p. to end.
5th row: K. across all sts.
6th row: P.
Now work as for right leg from *** to ***
Rib 1 row.
Next row: Cast off 44 (48; 50) sts., rib to end.
Complete as for right leg from **** to end.

TABS (Make 2)
With No. 11 (3 mm) needles and MS., cast on 7 sts. and work as folls.:
1st row: K. 2, (p. 1, k. 1) twice, k. 1.
2nd row: K. 1, (p. 1, k. 1) 3 times.
Rep. these 2 rows for 7 cm. (2½ in.).
Cast off.

MAKE UP
Do not press.
Join centre back and crotch seams, front crotch to ribbing and inside leg seam.
Attach tabs at sides and roll hem of legs and fasten tabs to hold in position.
Using siver cord lace front of jumpsuit as in photograph.
Position strap and adjust fit.

David Gower

CASUAL SWEATSHIRT

David Gower, England's cricket captain, loathes formal dress and prefers to be casual off the pitch in his own design for a sweatshirt-look pullover. His pet hate? Men who sport cricket sweaters without any intention of playing the game!

MATERIALS

Patons Moorland Tweed DK (**M**)	**50 g. balls**	11	11	12	12	12
Patons Moorland Shetland DK (**C**)	**50 g. balls**	1	1	1	1	1

Pair Milward needles each Nos. 8 (4 mm) and 10 (3¼ mm).
Set of four No. 10 (3¼ mm) needles.

MEASUREMENTS

To fit chest	**cm.**	91	97	102	107	112
	in.	36	38	40	42	44
Length from shoulder	**cm.**	65	66	67	68	69
	in.	25½	26	26½	26¾	27¼
Sleeve seam	**cm.**	51	51	51	51	51
	in.	20	20	20	20	20

TENSION
22 sts. and 30 rows to 10 cm. (4 in.) over reversed stocking stitch on No. 8 (4 mm) needles.

ABBREVIATIONS
k., knit; **p.**, purl; **sts.**, stitches; **rev.st.st.**, reversed stocking st.; **inc.**, increase, increasing; **dec.**, decrease, decreasing; **beg.**, beginning; **alt.**, alternate; **rep.**, repeat; **cm.**, centimetres; **in.**, inches; **M.**, main shade; **C.**, contrast.

FRONT
With No. 10 (3¼ mm) needles and C, cast on 99 (105; 111; 117; 123) sts.
1st row: K. 2, (p. 1, k. 1) to last st., k. 1.
2nd row: K. 1, (p. 1, k. 1) to end. Break C. Join in M.
Next row: K.
Beg. 2nd row continue in rib until work measures 10 cm. (4 in.), ending after a 1st row.**
Next row: Rib 5 (8; 6; 9; 6), *inc. in next st., rib 7 (7; 8; 8; 9); rep. from * to last 6 (9; 6; 9; 7) sts., inc. in next st., rib to end. 111 (117; 123; 129; 135) sts.
Change to No. 8 (4 mm) needles and beg. p. row work in rev.st.st. until front measures 48 (48; 49; 49; 50) cm., 19 (19; 19½; 19½; 19¾) in. from beg., ending after a p. row.
Divide for 'V' neck thus:–
Next row: K. 56 (59; 62; 65; 68), slip the last st. (centre st.) on a safety pin and leave, k. to end.
Continue on last group for left half.
***Dec. 1 st. at neck edge on next row, then on every following 3rd row until 46 (49; 52; 55; 58) sts. remain.
Work 3 rows straight. (N.B. on right half only work 4 rows straight).
Continue neck shaping by casting off 3 (4; 5; 6; 7) sts. at beg. of next row. Dec. 1 st. at neck edge on next 3 rows. 40 (42; 44; 46; 48) sts.
Work straight until front measures 65 (66; 67; 68; 69) cm., 25½ (26; 26½; 26¾; 27¼) in. from beg., ending at side edge.
Shape shoulder by casting off 13 (14; 15; 15; 16) sts. at beg. of next and following alt. row. Work 1 row. Cast off.
With right side facing, rejoin M. Complete as left half working from *** to end.

BACK
Omitting neck shaping work as front to shoulder shaping, ending after a k. row.
Shape shoulders by casting off 13 (14; 15; 15; 16) sts. at beg. of next 4 rows, then 14 (14; 14; 16; 16) sts. at beg. of next 2 rows. Slip final 31 (33; 35; 37; 39) sts. on a spare needle.

SLEEVES
With No. 10 (3¼ mm) needles and C, cast on 45 (47; 49; 51; 53) sts. Work as front to **.
Next row: K., inc. once in every st. 90 (94; 98; 102; 106) sts.
Next row: P. 3 (5; 4; 6; 3), *inc. in next st., p. 11 (11; 9; 9; 8); rep. from * to last 3 (5; 4; 6; 4) sts., inc. in next st., rib to end. 98 (102; 108; 112; 118) sts.
Change to No. 8 (4 mm) needles and beg. k. row (for wrong side) work in rev.st.st. until sleeve measures 51 cm. (20 in.). Cast off.

NECK INSET
With No. 10 (3¼ mm) needles and M, cast on 3 sts.
1st row: K. 1, p. 1, k. 1.
2nd row: P. 1, k. 1, p. 1.
Continue in k. 1, p. 1 rib, shaping sides by inc. 1 st. at each end of next row, then on every following 3rd row until there are 23 sts. Work 1 row. Slip sts. on a spare needle.

EDGING TO 'V' SECTION OF FRONT NECK
With No. 10 (3¼ mm) needles and C, k. up 26 sts. down left side of 'V' neck, k. 1 from safety pin, now k. up 26 sts. up right side of 'V' neck. (53 sts.)
Beg. 2nd row work 2 rows in rib as on welt, dec. 1 st. at either side of centre st. on both rows. Cast off evenly in rib.

NECKBAND
First join shoulders. With set of No. 10 (3¼ mm) needles and C, k. across sts. of back, k. up 21 (25; 25; 25; 29) sts. down left front neck (including contrast border), now k. across 23 sts. on spare needle, finally k. up 21 (25; 25; 25; 29) sts. up right front neck. 96 (106; 108; 110; 120) sts.
Work 2 rounds in k. 1, p. 1 rib. Break C. Join in M and k. 1 round. Work 7 more rounds in k. 1, p. 1 rib. Cast off evenly in rib.

TO MAKE UP
Omitting ribbing, press following pressing instructions. Stitch shaped edges of inset to contrast border of 'V' neck. Stitch cast-off edges of sleeves in position to yoke, allowing approximately 66 (68; 72; 74; 78) rows for armhole. Join side and sleeve seams. Press seams.

Eve Pollard

THE PLUNGING V

Eve Pollard is a favourite TV AM personality and talent spotter. She is married to Nicholas Lloyd, former editor of the News of the World. Eve is delightfully daring in her dress and here has chosen an ultra-conventional neutral shaded cricket-style sweater with an absolutely shocking cleavage.

MATERIALS

Patons Cotton Ribbon	**50 g. balls**	16	16	17	18

Pair Milward needles each Nos. 5 (5½ mm) and 8 (4 mm).
Set of four No. 8 (4 mm) needles.
Pair small shoulder pads.

MEASUREMENTS

To fit bust	**cm.**	81	86	91	97
	in.	32	34	36	38
Length from shoulder	**cm.**	62	63	65	66
	in.	24½	25	25½	26
Sleeve seam	**cm.**	43	43	43	43
	in.	17	17	17	17

TENSION

20 sts. and 24 rows to 10 cm. (4 in.) over pattern on No. 5 (5½ mm) needles.

ABBREVIATIONS

k., knit; **p.**, purl; **k.b.**, k. into back of next stitch; **sts.**, stitches; **patt.**, pattern; **inc.**, increase, increasing; **dec.**, decrease, decreasing; **tog.**, together; **beg.**, beginning; **alt.**, alternate; **rep.**, repeat; **cm.**, centimetres; **in.**, inches.

FRONT

With No. 8 (4 mm) needles, cast on 77 (81; 85; 89) sts.
1st row: K. 1, (k.b., p. 1) to last 2 sts., k.b., k. 1.
2nd row: K. 1, (p. 1, k. 1) to end.
Rep. these 2 rows for 10 cm. (4 in.), ending after a 2nd row and inc. 6 sts. evenly on last row. 83 (87; 91; 95) sts.
Change to No. 5 (5½ mm) needles and patt. thus:–
1st row: P. 2 (4; 6; 8), (k.b., p. 5) to last 3 (5; 7; 9) sts., k.b., p. to end.
2nd row: K.**
These 2 rows form patt.
Continue in patt. until work measures 36 cm. (14 in.) from beg., ending after a right-side row.
Keeping patt. correct, divide for 'V' neck thus:–
Next row: K. 42 (44; 46; 48), slip last st. on a safety pin, k. to end.
Continue on last group of sts.
Dec. 1 st. at neck edge on 3rd row following, then on every following 4th row until 37 (39; 41; 43) sts. remain.
Work 3 rows straight.
Shape armhole thus:–
Next row: Cast off 4 (5; 6; 7) sts., work to last 2 sts., work 2 tog.
Next row: Work to end.
***Work 5 rows dec. 1 st. at armhole edge on every right-side row and at neck edge on 3rd row only. 28 (29; 30; 31) sts.
Continue dec. at front edge only on 2nd row following, then on every following 4th row until 22 (22; 23; 23) sts. remain.
Work straight until front measures 19 (20; 21; 23) cm., 7½ (8; 8½; 9) in. from beg. of armhole shaping, ending at armhole edge:
Shape shoulder by casting off 7 (7; 8; 8) sts. at beg. of next and following alt. row.
Work 1 row. Cast off.
With right side facing, rejoin yarn to remaining sts.
Dec. 1 st. at neck edge on 3rd row following, then on every following 4th row until 36 (38; 40; 42) sts. remain.
Shape armhole thus:–
Next row: Cast off 4 (5; 6; 7) sts., work to end.
Complete as left half working from *** to end.

BACK

Work as front to **.
Continue in patt. until back measures same as front to armhole shaping, ending after a k. row.
Shape armholes by casting off 4 (5; 6; 7) sts. at beg. of next 2 rows. Dec. 1 st. at each end of next 3 right-side rows. 69 (71; 73; 75) sts.
Work straight until back measures same as front to shoulder shaping, ending after a p. row.
Shape shoulders by casting off 7 (7; 8; 8) sts. at beg. of next 4 rows, then 8 (8; 7; 7) sts. at beg. of next 2 rows. Slip final 25 (27; 27; 29) sts. on a spare needle.

SLEEVES

With No. 8 (4 mm) needles, cast on 39 (41; 41; 43) sts. Work in rib as on front for 10 cm. (4 in.), ending after a 1st row.
Next row: Rib 2 (2; 7; 6), *inc. in next st., rib 4 (3; 1; 1); rep. from * to last 2 (3; 8; 7) sts., inc. in next st., rib to end. 47 (51; 55; 59) sts.
Change to No. 5 (5½ mm) needles and patt. as on front, shaping sleeve by inc. 1 st. at each end of 5th row following, then on every following 6th row until there are 65 (69; 73; 77) sts., then on every following 4th row until there are 71 (75; 79; 83) sts., working extra sts. into patt.
Work straight until sleeve measures 43 cm. (17 in.) at centre, ending after a k. row.
Shape top by casting off 4 (5; 6; 7) sts. at beg. of next 2 rows. Dec. 1 st. at each end of next row, then on every following 4th row until 53 sts. remain, then on every following alt. row until 45 sts. remain, finally on every row until 39 sts. remain. Cast off.

NECKBAND

First join shoulders. With set of No. 8 (4 mm) needles and right side facing, k. across sts. of back, knit up 67 (69; 73; 75) sts. evenly down left front neck, k. 1 from safety-pin, finally knit up 67 (69; 73; 75) sts. up right front neck. 160 (166; 174; 180) sts.
Keeping centre front st. a "k." stitch on every round work in twisted rib as follows:
1st round: (P. 1, k.b.) to within 2 sts. of centre front st., p. 2 tog., k. 1, p. 2 tog., (k.b., p. 1) to last st., k. 1.
2nd round: P. 1, (k. 1, p. 1) to within 2 sts. of centre front st., k. 2 tog., k. 1, k. 2 tog., (p. 1, k. 1) to end.
Rep. these 2 rounds twice more then 1st round again. Cast off evenly in rib, dec. 1 st. either side of centre front st. as before.

TO MAKE UP

Do not press.
Join side and sleeve seams. Sew in sleeves easing in any extra fullness at top.
Insert shoulder pads.

Lysette Anthony
MINI TUNIC SUIT

Lysette Anthony, who was the most rescued – and rescuable – screen heroine we have seen for years in the sci-fi movie *Krull,* has also made a name for herself in television in *Auf Wiedersehen Pet.* Lysette dislikes clothes that encumber which is why she designed this most attractive outfit – a simple white mini skirt with a colourful, complementary tunic top.

MATERIALS

Patons Cotton Top, **Skirt**	**M** (White)	**50 g. balls**	5	5	6	6
Tunic,	**M** (White)	**50 g. balls**	8	8	9	9
	A (Turquoise)	**50 g. balls**	2	2	2	2
	B (Cerise)	**50 g. balls**	2	2	2	2

Pair Milward needles each Nos. 7 (4½ mm), 8 (4 mm), 9 (3¾ mm) and 10 (3¼ mm).
Length of elastic for skirt.

MEASUREMENTS

To fit hips	**cm.**	86	91	97	102
	in.	34	36	38	40
To fit bust	**cm.**	81	86	91	97
	in.	32	34	36	38
Skirt, length excluding waistband	**cm.**	48	48	48	48
	in.	19	19	19	19
Tunic, length	**cm.**	76	76	76	76
	in.	30	30	30	30
Sleeve seam	**cm.**	48	48	48	48
	in.	19	19	19	19

TENSION
20 sts. and 28 rows to 10 cm. (4 in.) over stocking stitch on No. 8 (4 mm) needles and 19 sts. and 27 rows to 10 cm. (4 in.) over stocking stitch on No. 7 (4½ mm) needles.

ABBREVIATIONS
k., knit; **p.**, purl; **sts.**, stitches; **st.st.**, stocking st.; **g.st.**, garter st.; **inc.**, increase, increasing; **dec.**, decrease, decreasing; **tog.**, together; **t.b.l.**, through back of loops; **beg.**, beginning; **patt.**, pattern; **rep.**, repeat; **cm.**, centimetres; **in.**, inches; **M**, white; **A**, turquoise; **B**, cerise.

SKIRT
Front and back (2 pieces alike)
With No. 10 (3¼ mm) needles and M, cast on 97 (102; 107; 112) sts.
Work 7 rows in g.st. inc. 9 sts. evenly on last row. 106 (111; 116; 121) sts.
Change to No. 8 (4 mm) needles and beg. k. row work 12 rows in st.st.
Shape skirt thus:–
Dec. row: K. 24, k. 2 tog. t.b.l., k. to last 26 sts., k. 2 tog., k. 24.
Work 9 rows straight.
Rep. the last 10 rows until 90 (95; 100; 105) sts. remain.
Work straight until skirt measures 36 cm. (14 in.) from beg., ending after a p. row.
Shape hips by working dec. row as before on next row, then on every following 10th row until 82 (87; 92; 97) sts. remain.
Work 3 rows straight dec. 5 (4; 5; 4) sts. evenly on last row. 77 (83; 87; 93) sts.
Change to No. 10 (3¼ mm) needles and rib thus:–
1st row: K. 2, (p. 1, k. 1) to last st., k. 1.
2nd row: K. 1, (p. 1, k. 1) to end.
Work 6 more rows in rib. Cast off *loosely* in rib.

TO MAKE UP
Omitting ribbing, press following pressing instructions. Join side seams. Cut elastic to fit waist and join in a ring. Sew to inside waist ribbing using a herringbone stitch over the elastic to form a casing. Press seams.

TUNIC
Back and front (2 pieces alike)
With No. 9 (3¾ mm) needles and M, cast on 80 (84; 88; 92) sts.
Work 7 rows in g.st. inc. 8 sts. evenly on last row. 88 (92; 96; 100) sts.
Change to No. 7 (4½ mm) needles and beg. k. row work 14 rows in st.st.
Continue in st.st. working in patt. from charts thus:–
(N.B.: Use a separate ball of yarn for each colour area, twisting yarns on wrong side when changing colour to avoid a hole).
1st row: K. 28 (32; 36; 40) M, work 1st row of chart 1.
2nd row: Work 2nd row of chart 1, p. to end.
3rd to 48th rows: Rep. 1st and 2nd rows 23 times but working rows 3 to 48 from chart 1.
Work 8 rows all in M.
Work from chart 2 thus:–
1st row: Work 1st row from chart 2, k. 18 (22; 26; 30) M.
2nd row: P. 18 (22; 26; 30) M, work 2nd row from chart 2.
3rd to 50th rows: Rep. 1st and 2nd rows 24 times but working rows 3 to 50 from chart 2.
Work 8 rows all in M.
Work from chart 3 thus:–
1st row: K. 13 (17; 21; 25) M, work 1st row from chart 3.
2nd row: Work 2nd row from chart 3, p. to end.
3rd to 44th rows: Rep. 1st and 2nd rows 21 times but working rows 3 to 44 from chart 3.
Break A and B. Continue in M until work measures 71 cm. (28 in.) at centre, ending after a p. row.
Change to No. 9 (3¾ mm) needles and rib as on skirt waistband for 5 cm. (2 in.).
Cast off evenly in rib.

Sleeves
With No. 9 (3¾ mm) needles and M, cast on 35 (37; 39; 41) sts. Work in rib as on skirt waistband for 7 cm. (3 in.), ending after a 2nd row.
Next row: K. inc. once in every st. 70 (74; 78; 82) sts.
Next row: P. inc. 6 sts. evenly across. 76 (80; 84; 88) sts.
Change to No. 7 (4½ mm) needles and beg. k. row work 2 rows in st.st.
Continue in st.st. working in patt. from charts thus:–
1st row: K. 16 (20; 24; 28) M, work 1st row of chart 1.
2nd row: Work 2nd row of chart 1, p. to end.
3rd to 48th rows: Rep. 1st and 2nd rows 23 times working rows 3 to 48 of chart 1.
Work 2 rows all in M.
Work from chart 2 thus:–
1st row: Work 1st row from chart 2, k. 6 (10; 14; 18).

2nd row: P. 6 (10; 14; 18), work 2nd row from chart 2.
3rd to 50th rows: Rep. 1st and 2nd rows 24 times but working rows 3 to 50 from chart 2. Work 2 rows all in M. Cast off loosely in M.

TO MAKE UP

Press as skirt. Leaving approximately 44 centre sts. free, join shoulders. Allowing approximately 54 (57; 60; 63) rows for armhole, stitch cast-off edges of sleeves in position to yoke. Join side and sleeve seams. Press seams.

KEY
(FOR ALL CHARTS)

□ = M (white)
× = A (turquoise)
● = B (cerise)

Read odd rows "k." from right to left and even rows "p." from left to right.

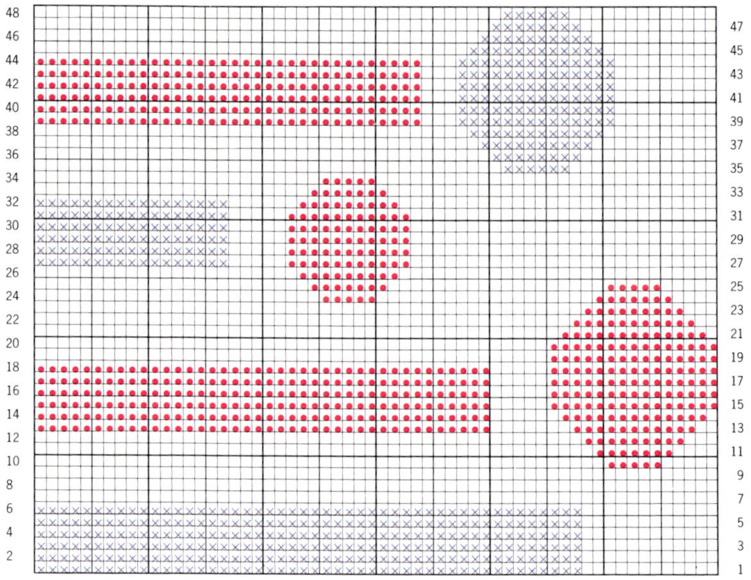

CHART 1 60 pattern stitches

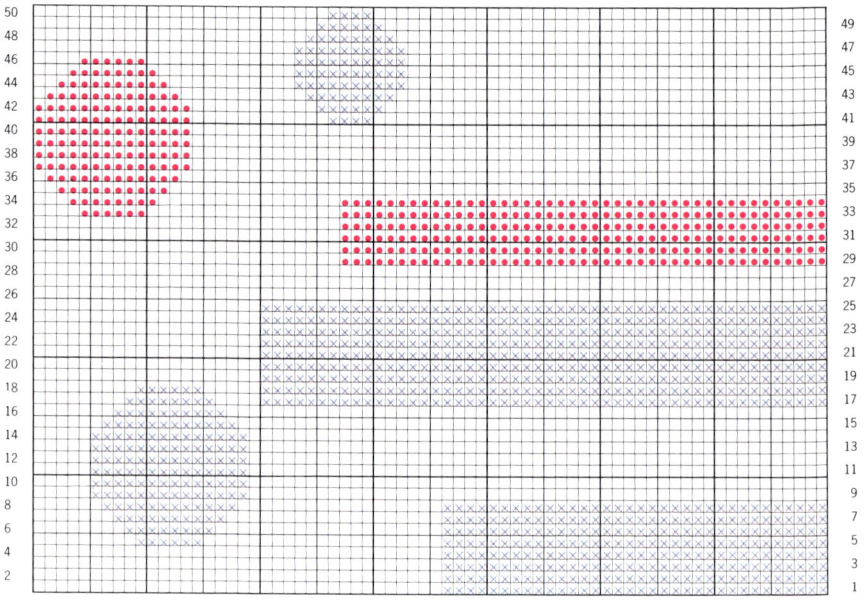

CHART 2 70 pattern stitches

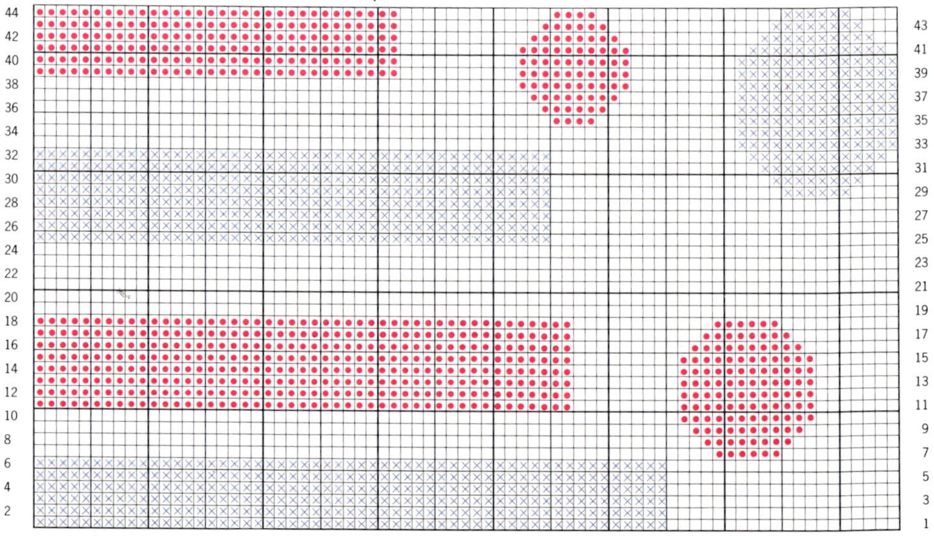

CHART 3 75 pattern stitches

Geraldine James

COUNTY-LOOK GEOMETRIC PATTERNED COAT

Geraldine James who was such a hit as the thoroughly decent Sarah Layton in *Jewel In The Crown* has scored another success as Lady Maud in Tom Sharpe's *Blott On The Landscape.* This well cut, casual wrap coat brings out her glowing physical appeal. Instant streamlining is an added advantage because Geraldine was six months pregnant when photographed.

MATERIALS

A (Patons Siberia Shade 2183)	**50 g. balls**	3
B (Patons Siberia Shade 2188)	**50 g. balls**	2
C (Patons Beehive Chunky Shade 9174)	**50 g. balls**	3
D (Patons Beehive Chunky Shade 9351)	**50 g. balls**	5
E (Patons Solo Chunky Shade 2254)	**50 g. balls**	2
F (Patons Diana Shade 9209)	**50 g. balls**	3
G (Patons Stonewash Ribbon Shade 2283)	**50 g. balls**	3
H (Patons Stonewash Ribbon Shade 2266)	**50 g. balls**	3
J (Patons Stonewash Ribbon Shade 2277)	**50 g. balls**	2

Pair each No. 6 (5 mm) and No. 5 (5½ mm) Knitting needles. A No. 7 (4.50 mm) crocket hook.

MEASUREMENTS

One Size To Fit 81–97 cm. (32–38 in.).
Length approx 101 cm. (40 in.).
Sleeve seam approx. 16 cm. (6 in.).

TENSION

15 sts. and 20 rows to 10 cm. (4 in.) measured over st.st. on No. 5 (5½ mm) needles using A.

ABBREVIATIONS

k., knit; **p.**, purl; **st.**, stitch; **st.st.**, stocking stitch; **rev.**, reverse; **beg.**, beginning; **alt.**, alternate; **rep.**, repeat; **patt.**, pattern; **cont.**, continue; **foll.**, following; **rem.**, remaining; **r.s.**, right side; **w.s.**, wrong side; **cm.**, centimetres; **mm.**, millimetres; **in.**, inches; **MB.**, (on r.s. row), make bobble as folls.; (using yarn as given on key), [k. 1, p. 1] twice into next st., p. 4, turn, k. 4 turn, [p. 2 tog.] twice, turn k. 2 tog.; thus completing bobble; **MB.** (on w.s. row), make bobble as folls.: (using yarn as given on key), [k. 1, p. 1] twice into next st. k. 4, turn p. 4, turn, [k. 2 tog.] twice, turn, p. 2 tog.; thus completing bobble.

SPECIAL NOTES

Use separate balls of yarn for each section as indicated, twisting yarns on w.s. to avoid a hole. Heavy black lines indicate outline of each area. Areas are worked in either st.st. (k. on r.s., p. on w.s.) or rev.st.st. (p. on r.s., k. on w.s.) as given on key.
Symbols indicate position of bobbles, these are worked in the yarn as given on key.
Take care when working from chart to read instructions correctly as the chart is turned various ways to give the unusual pattern to this coat.

LEFT FRONT

**With No. 6 (5 mm) needles and D, cast on 67 sts. and k. 3 rows.
Change to No. 5 (5½ mm) needles and joining in and breaking off colours, work in patt. from chart for 192 rows.
Shape shoulder, keeping patt. correct, by casting off 12 sts. at beg. of next and foll. 3 alt. rows.
Work 1 row, thus ending with r.s. facing.**
Cont. in patt. on rem. 19 sts. for 26 rows, this forms collar.
Cast off.

RIGHT FRONT
**With No. 6 (5 mm) needles and D, cast on 67 sts. and k. 3 rows.
Change to No. 5 (5½ mm) needles and joining in and breaking off colours, turn chart upside down thereby starting with 100th row and working through to 1st row, work as for left front, reversing shapings.**

RIGHT BACK
Work as for left front from ** to **.
Cast off rem. 19 sts.

LEFT BACK
Work as for right front from ** to **, omitting collar and casting off rem. 19 sts.

SLEEVES
With No. 6 (5 mm) needles and E, cast on 100 sts. and k. 3 rows.
Change to No. 5 (5½ mm) needles and joining in and breaking off colours, turn chart on its side as marked and work 30 rows.
Cast off. Place two markers on cast off edge of sleeves, 5 cm. (2 in.) in from side edges.

MAKE UP
Do not press.
Join centre back seam, leaving lower 30 cm. (12 in.) open.
Join shoulder seams, sewing extra 26 rows from front to 19 sts of back neck, join collar pieces as centre back.
Using No. 7 (4.50 mm) crochet hook and D, work 2 rows of double crochet around front edges and collar.
Place markers 38 rows below shoulders on front edges.
Fold collar in half at centre back and graduate away down to markers on centre front edges.
Stitch collar in position.
Place centre of sleeve to shoulder and sew in leaving 5 cm. (2 in.) (as marked) either side of underarm free.
Join underarm seam.
Using No. 7 (4.50 mm) crocket hook and D, work 2 rows of double crochet around side edges and underarm and centre back slit.

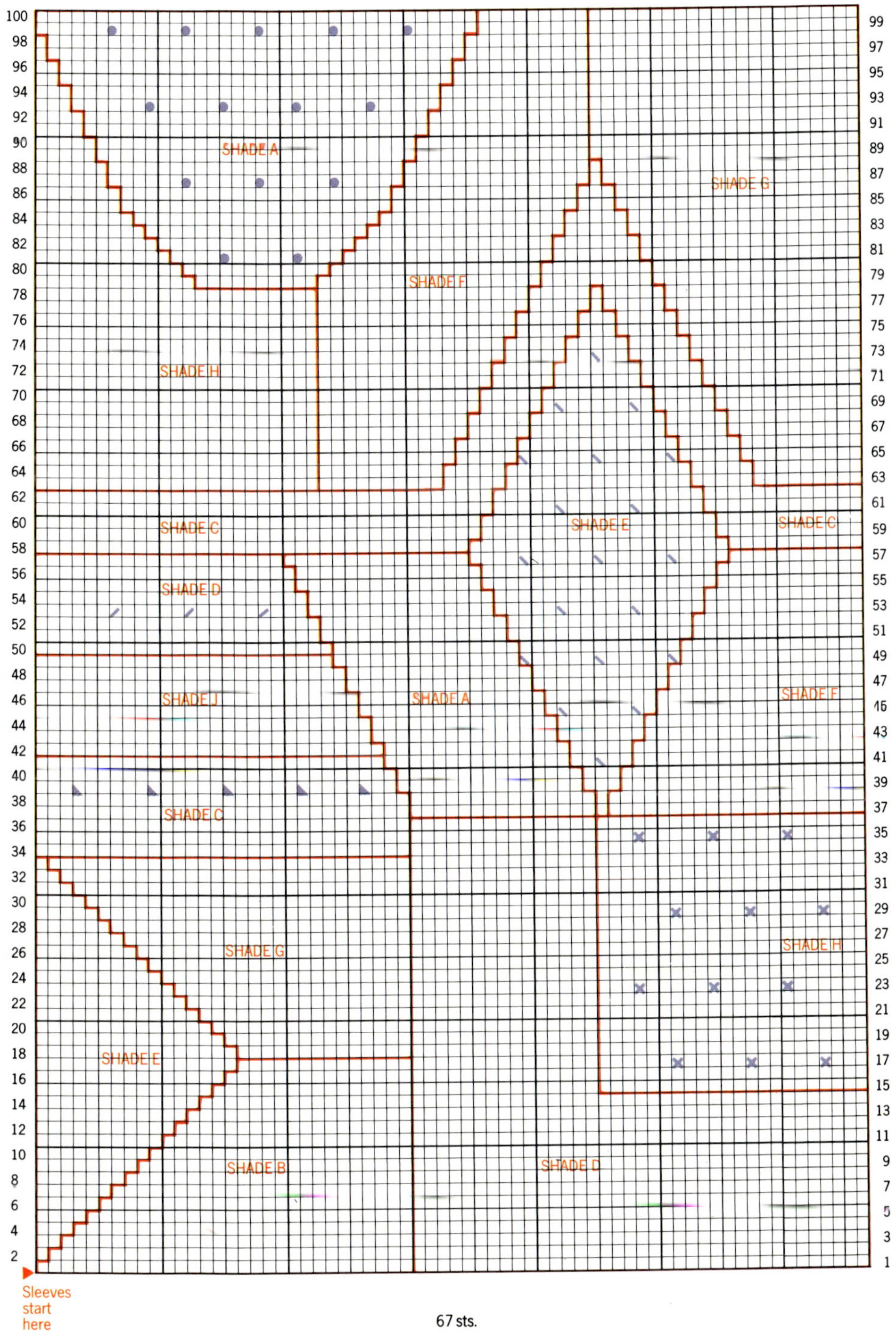

KEY

A work in rev.st.st.
B work in st.st.
C work in st.st.
D work in st.st.
E work in rev.st.st.
F work in st.st.
G work in rev.st.st.
H work in rev.st.st.
J work in rev.st.st.

= MB. using A;
= MB. using C;
= MB. using D;
= MB. using H;
= MB. using J;

Barbara Hulanicki

WHITE ON WHITE STUNNER

The hand that rocked the Sixties, and ruled the fashion world with her Biba designs, continues to create favourites the Eighties with this flattering cool cotton outfit especially for you. This is the suit which makes every woman look like she wants to look.

MATERIALS

Patons Cotton Soft, **Jacket**	**50 g. balls**	13	13	14
Skirt	**50 g. balls**	12	12	13

Jacket: Pair Milward needles each Nos. 8 (4 mm) and 10 (3¼ mm). 4 buttons.
Skirt: Pair Milward needles each Nos. 9 (3¾ mm) and 11 (3 mm). Length of 2 cm. (1 in.) elastic to fit waist for skirt

MEASUREMENTS

To fit bust	**cm.**	81	86	91
	in.	32	34	36
Jacket, length from shoulder	**cm.**	71	72	74
	in.	28	28½	29
Sleeve seam	**cm.**	42	42	42
	in.	16½	16½	16½
Skirt, to fit hips	**cm.**	86	91	97
	in.	34	36	38
Length, excluding waistband	**cm.**	84	84	84
	in.	33	33	33

TENSION
22 sts. and 29 rows to 10 cm. (4 in.) over reversed stocking stitch on No. 8 (4 mm) needles and 23 sts. and 30 rows to 10 cm. (4 in.) over reversed stocking stitch on No. 9 (3¾ mm) needles.

ABBREVIATIONS
k., knit; **p.**, purl; **sts.**, stitches; **g.st.**, garter st.; **rev.st.st.**, reversed stocking st.; **m.1**, make 1 by picking up and knitting into back of horizontal strand lying before next st.; **inc.**, increase, increasing; **dec.**, decrease, decreasing; **beg.**, beginning; **alt.**, alternate; **tog.**, together; **cm.**, centimetres; **in.**, inches.

JACKET
Back
With No. 10 (3¼ mm) needles, cast on 89 (95; 101) sts.
1st row: K. 2, (p. 1, k. 1) to last st., k. 1.
2nd row: K. 1, (p. 1, k. 1) to end.
Work 18 more rows in rib inc. 8 sts. evenly on last row. 97 (103; 109) sts.
Change to No. 8 (4 mm) needles and beg. p. row work 120 rows in rev.st.st.
Shape armholes by casting off 5 (6; 7) sts. at beg. of next 2 rows.
Dec. 1 st. at each end of next 3 rows, then on the following alt. rows. 77 (81; 85) sts.
Work straight until back measures 23 (24; 25) cm., 9 (9½; 10) in. firom beg. of armhole shaping, measured through centre of work and ending after a p. row.
Shape shoulders by casting off 8 sts. at beg. of next 4 rows, then 7 (8; 9) sts. at beg. of next 2 rows. Cast off final 31 (33; 35) sts.

Pocket Linings (2)
With No. 8 (4 mm) needles, cast on 33 sts. loosely. Beg. p. row work 32 rows in rev.st.st. Slip sts. on a spare needle.

Right Front
With No. 10 (3¼ mm) needles, cast on 43 (45; 49) sts. Work 20 rows in rib as on back but inc. 4 (5; 4) sts. evenly on last row. 47 (50; 53) sts.
Change to No. 8 (4 mm) needles and beg. p. row work 32 rows in rev.st.st.
Place pocket lining thus:
Next row: P. 7 (8; 9), slip next 33 sts. on a spare needle and in place of these p. across a group of lining sts., p. to end.
Work 17 rows.
Shape front slope by dec. 1 st. at front edge on next row, then on every following 8th row until 38 (41; 44) sts. remain.
Work 6 rows straight. (**N.B.**: Work 5 rows only here on left front).
Shape armhole thus:
Next row: Cast off 5 (6; 7) sts., work to end.
(**N.B.:** On left front only, now k. 1 row).
Dec. 1 st. at armhole edge on next 3 rows, then on the 2 following alt. rows, at the same time dec. 1 st. at front edge on 1st row. 27 (29; 31) sts.
Continue dec. at front edge only on 4th row following, then on every following 10th row until 23 (24; 25) sts. remain.
Work straight until front measures same as back to shoulder shaping, ending at armhole edge.
Shape shoulder by casting off 8 sts. at beg. of next and following alt. row. Work 1 row. Cast off.

Left Front
Work as given for right front but noting that pocket row will commence 'p. 7 (9; 11)'.

Sleeves
With No. 10 (3¼ mm) needles, cast on 48 (52; 55) sts. Work 5 rows in g.st. inc. 3 (3; 4) sts. evenly on last row. 51 (55; 59) sts.
Change to No. 8 (4 mm) needles and beg. p. row work in rev.st.st., shaping sleeve by inc. 1 st. at each end of 1st row, then on every following 7th row until there are 77 (81; 85) sts. Work straight until sleeve measures 34 cm. (13½ in.) from beg., ending after a k. row.
Continue shaping by inc. 1 st. at each end of next row, then on every following 3rd row until there are 91 (95; 99) sts.
Work 3 rows straight.
Shape top by casting off 5 (6; 7) sts. at beg. of next 2 rows.
Work 0 (2; 4) rows straight.
Dec. 1 st. at each end of every p. row until 55 sts. remain, then on every row until 45 sts. remain. Cast off.

Pocket Tops
With right side facing, slip a group of pocket sts. onto a No. 10 (3¼ mm) needle.
Beg. 2nd row work 6 rows in rib as on welt. Cast off evenly in rib.

Borders
With No. 10 (3¼ mm) needles, cast on 11 sts. Work a strip in rib to fit up front edge and round to centre back of neck when slightly stretched. Cast off in rib.
Mark position on border for 4 buttons, 1st to be

between 3rd/4th rows, last one level with or a little below start of front slope and remaining 2 spaced evenly between.
Work 2nd strip as first but working holes to match markers thus:
1st row: Rib 4, cast off 3 sts. in rib, rib to end.
2nd row: In rib casting on 3 over those cast off.

TO MAKE UP
Do not press. Sew down pocket linings on wrong side and tops on right side. Join shoulder, side and sleeve seams. Sew in sleeves. Sew on borders joining ends at back of neck. Sew on buttons.

SKIRT
Front and Back (2 pieces alike)
With No. 11 (3 mm) needles, cast on 154 (160; 166) sts.
Work 4 rows in g.st.
Next row: K. 2 (5; 8), (m.1, k. 15) 10 times, m.1, k. to end. 165 (171; 177) sts.
Change to No. 9 (3¾ mm) needles and rev.st.st. with 'rib' gores thus:
1st row: P. 10 (13; 16), (k. 1, p. 23) 6 times, k. 1, p. 10 (13; 16).
2nd row: K. 10 (13; 16), (p. 1, k. 23) 6 times, p. 1, k. 10 (13; 16).
These 2 rows form pattern.
Work 44 more rows.
Shape skirt thus:
1st dec. row: P. 1, p. 2 tog., p. 7 (10; 13), (k. 1, p. 10, p. 3 tog., p. 10) 6 times, k. 1 p. to last 3 sts., p. 2 tog., p. 1. 151 (157; 163) sts.
Keeping ribs correct, work 47 rows straight.
2nd dec. row: P. 1, p. 2 tog., p. 6 (9; 12), (k. 1, p. 9, p. 3 tog., p. 9) 6 times, k. 1, p. to last 3 sts., p. 2 tog., p. 1. 137 (143; 149) sts.
Work 47 rows straight.
3rd dec. row: P. 1, p. 2 tog., p. 5 (8; 11), k. 1, p. 8, p. 3 tog., p. 8) 6 times, k. 1, p. to last 3 sts., p. 2 tog., p. 1. 123 (129; 135) sts.
Work 47 rows straight.
4th dec. row: P. 1, p. 2 tog., p. 4 (7; 10), (k. 1, p. 7, p. 3 tog., p. 7) 6 times, k. 1, p. to last 3 sts., p. 2 tog., p. 1. 109 (115; 121) sts.
Work straight until skirt measures 71 cm. (28 in.) at centre, ending after a wrong-side row.
Shape hips thus:
1st dec. row: P. 1, p. 2 tog., p. 3 (6; 9), (k. 1, p. 6, p. 3 tog., p. 6) 6 times, k. 1, p. to last 3 sts., p. 2 tog., p. 1. 95 (101; 107) sts.
Work 27 rows straight.
2nd dec. row: P. 1, p. 2 tog., p. 2 (5; 8), (k. 1, p. 5, p. 3 tog., p. 5) 6 times, k. 1, p. to last 3 sts., p. 2 tog., p. 1. 81 (87; 93) sts.
Work 7 rows straight.
Change to No. 11 (3 mm) needles and work 8 rows in rib as on back of jacket. Cast off *very loosely* in rib.

TO MAKE UP
Do not press. Join side seams. Cut elastic to fit waist and join in a ring. Sew to inside of waist ribbing using a herringbone stitch over the elastic to form a casing.

Sharron Davies

LONG, LOOSE V NECK

Sharron Davies, golden girl runner up in the Moscow Olympics and winner of the double Commonwealth gold in Edmonton now runs her own fashion business and is seen at all the right premieres. This loose, pale and elegant top is perfect for a hard-working girl who wants a smart but casual style.

MATERIALS

Patons Solo Chunky	**50 g. balls**	13	13	14	14	14

Pair Milward needles each Nos. 3 (6½ mm) and 5 (5½ mm).
Set of four No. 5 (5½ mm) needles

MEASUREMENTS

To fit bust	**cm.**	81	86	91	97	102
	in.	32	34	36	38	40
Actual width at underarms,	**cm.**	117	122	127	132	137
approximately	**in.**	46	48	50	52	54
Length from shoulder	**cm.**	76	77	77	79	79
	in.	30	30½	30½	31	31
Sleeve length at centre	**cm.**	47	47	47	47	47
	in.	18½	18½	18½	18½	18½

TENSION

14 sts. and 18 rows to 10 cm. (4 in.) over reversed stocking stitch on No. 3 (6½ mm) needles.

ABBREVIATIONS

k., knit; **p.**, purl; **sts.**, stitches; **rev.st.st.**, reversed stocking st.; **inc.**, increase, increasing; **dec.**, decrease, decreasing; **beg.**, beginning; **alt.**, alternate; **rep.**, repeat; **cm.** centimetres; **in.**, inches.

BACK

With No. 5 (5½ mm) needles, cast on 59 (63; 67; 71; 75) sts.
1st row: K. 2, (p. 1, k. 1) to last st., k. 1.
2nd row: K. 1, (p. 1, k. 1) to end.
Rep. these 2 rows for 11 cm. (4½ in.), ending after a 1st row.
Next row: Rib 3 (5; 7; 9; 11), (inc. in next st., rib 1, inc. in next st., rib 2) 11 times, rib to end. 81 (85; 89; 93; 97) sts.
Change to No. 3 (6½ mm) needles and beg. p. row work in rev.st.st. until back measures 76 (77; 77; 79; 79) cm., 30 (30½; 30½; 31; 31) in. from beg., ending after a k. row.
Shape shoulders by casting off 10 (11; 11; 12; 12) sts. at beg. of next 4 rows, then 10 (10; 11; 11; 12) sts. at beg. of next 2 rows. Slip final 21 (21; 23; 23; 25) sts. on a spare needle.

FRONT

Work as back until front measures 53 cm. (21 in.), ending after a p. row.
Divide for 'V' neck thus:–
Next row: K. 41 (43; 45; 47; 49), slip last st. (centre st.) on a safety pin and leave, k. to end.
Continue on last group. Dec. 1 st. at neck edge on 3rd row following, then on every following p. row until 35 (39; 38; 41; 42) sts. remain, then on every following 4th row until 30 (32; 33; 35; 36) sts. remain.
Work straight until front measures same as back to shoulder shaping, ending at side edge.
Shape shoulder by casting off 10 (11; 11; 12; 12) sts. at beg. of next and following alt. row. Work 1 row. Cast off.
With right side facing, rejoin yarn to remaining sts. and complete as first half.

SLEEVES

With No. 5 (5½ mm) needles, cast on 25 (27; 27; 29; 29) sts.
Work in rib as on back for 6 cm. (2½ in.), ending after a 1st row.
Next row: Rib 4 (4; 2; 3; 1), inc. once in next 16 (18; 22; 22; 26) sts., rib to end. 41 (45; 49; 51; 55) sts.
Change to No. 3 (6½ mm) needles and beg. p. row work in rev.st.st., shaping sleeve by inc. 1 st. at each end of 5th row, then on every following 4th row until there are 49 (53; 57; 59; 63) sts., then on every following 6th row until there are 65 (69; 73; 75; 79) sts.
Work straight until sleeve measures 47 cm. (18½ in.) at centre. Cast off loosely.

NECKBAND

First join shoulders. With set of No. 5 (5½ mm) needles, right side facing, k. across sts. of back, k. up 44 (46; 46; 48; 50) sts. evenly down left front neck, k. 1 from safety pin, finally k. up 44 (46; 46; 48; 50) sts. evenly up right front neck. 110 (114; 116; 120; 126) sts.
Keeping centre front st. a "k." st. on every round, work 6 rounds in k.1, p. 1 rib dec. 1 st. at each side of centre st. on every round. Cast off evenly in rib.

TO MAKE UP

Do not press. Stitch cast-off edges of sleeves to yoke allowing approximately 42 (44; 46; 48; 50) rows for armholes. Join side and sleeve seams.

Thomas & Co.

SIX BRIGHT SWEATERS AND ACCESSORIES

Thomas Hope, Hugh Sington, Hannah Nana, Katie Corcoran, Dido Xenakis, and Luke Wilson proudly show off their newly knitted sweaters. Thomas wears the nippy blue sweater with the big white spots. Hugh is in the vivid and pretty Fair Isle. Hannah wears the polo neck in three-colour checkerboard pattern and Katie the stripey, sporty crew necked sweater. Dido looks cute in her pale creamy polo neck, as does Luke wearing a yellow version of the same.

CABLE PANELLED WITH POLO COLLAR

MATERIALS

Patons Beehive DK	**50 g. balls**	4	5	5

Pair each Nos. 10 (3¼ mm) and 8 (4 mm) needles.

MEASUREMENTS

To fit chest	**cm.**	56	61	66
	in.	22	24	26
Length from top of shoulders	**cm.**	38	42	46
	in.	15	16½	18
Sleeve seam	**cm.**	28	30	33
	in.	11	12	13

TENSION

Pattern is based on a standard stocking stitch tension of 22 sts. and 30 rows measured over 10 cm. (4 in.) on No. 8 (4 mm) needles.

ABBREVIATIONS

k., knit; **p.**, purl; **sts.**, stitches; **mm.**, millimetres; **cm.**, centimetres; **in.**, inches; **rep.**, repeat; **m.1**, pick up horizontal loop lying before next st. and work into back of it; **C.8 F.**, slip next 4 sts. on cable needle to front of work, k. 4, then k. 4 from cable needle; **patt.**, pattern; **beg.**, beginning; **dec.**, decrease by working 2 sts. together.

BACK

**With No. 10 (3¼ mm) needles, cast on 55 (61; 67) sts.
1st row: Right side facing, k. 1, * p. 1, k. 1; rep. from * to end.
2nd row: P. 1, * k. 1, p. 1; rep. from * to end.
Rep. last 2 rows until back measures 5 cm. (2 in.), ending with 1st row.
Next row: Rib 1 (4; 7), m.1, * rib 2, m.1; rep. from * to last 2 (5; 8) sts., rib 2 (5; 8). 82 (88; 94) sts.
Change to No. 8 (4 mm) needles and work in cable patt. as follows:
1st row: Right side facing, p. 7 (8; 9), * k. 8, p. 7 (8; 9); rep. from * to end.
2nd row: K. 7 (8; 9), * p. 8, k. 7 (8; 9); rep. from * to end.
3rd and 4th rows: As 1st and 2nd.
5th row: P. 7 (8; 9), * C.8 F., p. 7 (8; 9); rep. from * to end.
6th row: As 2nd.
7th to 10th rows: As 1st and 2nd rows twice.
These 10 rows form patt.
Work straight in patt. until back measures 23 (27; 29) cm. 9 (10½; 11½) in. at centre from start, ending with right side facing. Place a marker at each end of last row. **
Continue in patt. until back measures 38 (42; 46) cm. 15 (16½; 18) in. at centre from start, ending with right side facing.
Shape shoulders by casting off 8 (8; 10) sts. at beg. of next 2 rows, then 8 (9; 9) sts. at beg. of next 4 rows. Leave remaining 34 (36; 38) sts. on a spare needle.

FRONT

Work as for back from ** to **.
Continue in patt. until front measures 34 (38; 42) cm. 13½ (15; 16½) in. at centre from start, ending with right side facing.
Here divide for neck.
Next row: Patt. 32 (34; 36), turn and leave remaining sts. on a spare needle.
Continue on these 32 (34; 36) sts. for first side, dec. 1 st. at neck edge on every row until 24 (26; 28) sts. remain.
Continue straight until front matches back to start of shoulder shaping, ending with right side facing.
Shape shoulder by casting off 8 (8; 10) sts. at beg. of next row, then 8 (9; 9) sts. at beg. of following 2 alternate rows.
With right side facing, slip centre 18 (20; 22) sts. on a spare needle, rejoin yarn to remaining sts., patt. to end. Finish to correspond with first side.

SLEEVES

With No. 10 (3¼ mm) needles, cast on 35 (35; 39) sts. and work 5 cm. (2 in.) k. 1, p. 1 rib, as for back, ending with 1st row.
Continue as follows:

1st and 2nd sizes only:
Next row: (Work into front and back of next st., m.1) twice, * rib 1, m.1; rep. from * to last 2 sts., work into front and back of next st., m.1, work into front and back of last st. 72 (72) sts.

3rd size only:
Next row: Rib 1, + m.1, rib 1; rep. from * to end. 77 sts.

All sizes:
Change to No. 8 (4 mm) needles and work in patt. placing cable panels as follows:
1st row: Right side facing, p. 8 (8; 9), * k. 8, p. 8 (8; 9); rep. from * to end.
Continue in cable patt. thus until sleeve measures 28 (30; 33) cm. 11 (12; 13) in. at centre from start, ending with right side facing. Cast off loosely in patt.

COLLAR

Join right shoulder seam.
With right side facing and No. 10 (3¼ mm) needles, start at left shoulder on front and pick up and k. 16 sts. down left side of neck, k. 18 (20; 22) from centre, pick up and k. 16 up right side, then k. 34 (36; 38) from back. 84 (88; 92) sts.
Work 11 (13; 14) cm. 4½ (5; 5½) in. k. 1, p. 1 rib.
Cast off loosely in rib, using a bigger needle.

TO MAKE UP

Do not press. Join left shoulder seam, and collar. Join side and sleeve seams; insert sleeves.

CREW NECK WITH SPOTTED YOKE

MATERIALS

Patons Cotton Perle (**MS**)	**50 g. balls**	5	6	6
(**C**)	**50 g. balls**	1	1	1

Pair each Nos. 10 (3¼ mm) and 8 (4 mm) needles

MEASUREMENTS

To fit chest	**cm.**	56	61	66
	in.	22	24	26
Length from top of shoulders	**cm.**	38	42	46
	in.	15	16½	18
Sleeve seam	**cm.**	28	30	33
	in.	11	12	13

TENSION

22 sts. and 29 rows measured over 10 cm. (4 in.) of stocking stitch on No. 8 (4 mm) needles.

ABBREVIATIONS

k., knit; **p.**, purl; **sts.**, stitches; **st.st.**, stocking st.; **mm.**, millimetres; **cm.**, centimetres; **in.**, inches; **rep.**, repeat; **patt.**, pattern; **beg.**, beginning; **dec.**, decrease by working 2 sts. together; **inc.**, increase by working into front and back of st.; **m.1**, pick up horizontal loop lying before next st. and work into back of it; **MS**, Main Shade; **C**, Contrast.

BACK

**With No. 10 (3¼ mm) needles and MS, cast on 55 (61; 67) sts.

1st row: Right side facing, k. 1, * p. 1, k. 1; rep. from * to end.

2nd row: P. 1, * k. 1, p. 1; rep. from * to end.

Rep. last 2 rows until work measures 5 cm. (2 in.) ending with 1st row.

Next row: Rib 5 (8; 3), m.1, * rib 3 (3; 4), m.1; rep. from * to last 5 (8; 4) sts., rib 5 (8; 4). 71 (77; 83) sts.

Change to No. 8 (4 mm) needles and st.st., starting with a k. row, and work straight until back measures 23 (27; 29) cm. 9 (10½; 11½) in. at centre from start, ending with a p. row. Place a marker at each end of last row. **

Change to patt. for yoke as follows:

1st row: Right side facing, k. 6 (9; 12) MS, join in a 125 cm. (49 in.) length of C yarn and k. 3 C, * k. 11 MS, join in a 125 cm. (49 in.) length of C. yarn and k. 3 C; rep. from * to last 6 (9; 12) sts., k. 6 (9; 12) MS.

2nd row: P. 5 (8; 11) MS, 5 C, * 9 MS, 5 C; rep. from * to last 5 (8; 11) sts., 5 (8; 11) MS.

N.B.: Twist yarns at back of work when changing colour to avoid a hole.

3rd row: K., 4 (7; 10) MS, 7 C, * 7 MS, 7 C; rep. from * to last 4 (7; 10) sts., 4 (7; 10) MS.

4th row: As 3rd, but reading 'p.' for 'k.' throughout.

5th and 6th rows: As 3rd and 4th.

7th row: As 3rd.

8th row: As 2nd.

9th row: As 1st, but omitting joining in of yarn.

10th row: P. in MS.

11th row: K. 13 (16; 5) MS, join in a 125 cm. (49 in.) length of C yarn and k. 3 C, * k. 11 MS, join in a 125 cm. (49 in.) length of C yarn and k. 3 C; rep. from * to last 13 (16; 5) sts., k. 13 (16; 5) MS.
12th row: P., 12 (15; 4) MS, 5 C, * 9 MS, 5 C; rep. from * to last 12 (15; 4) sts., 12 (15; 4) MS.
13th row: K. 11 (14; 3) MS, 7 C, * 7 MS, 7 C; rep. from * to last 11 (14; 3) sts., 11 (14; 3) MS.
14th row: As 13th, but reading 'p.' for 'k.' throughout.
15th and 16th rows: As 13th and 14th.
17th row: As 13th.
18th row: As 12th.
19th row: As 11th, but omitting joining in of yarns.
20th row: P. in MS.
These 20 rows form patt. for yoke. **
Continue straight in patt. until back measures 38 (42; 46) cm. 16 (16½; 18) in., ending with a p. row.
Shape shoulders by casting off 8 (8; 8) sts. at beg. of next 2 rows, then 7 (8; 9) sts. at beg. of next 4 rows. Leave remaining 27 (29; 31) sts. on a spare needle.

FRONT
Work as for back from ** to **.
Continue straight in patt. until front measures 34 (38; 42) cm. 13½ (15; 16½) in. at centre from start, ending with right side facing.
Here divide for neck.
Next row: Patt. 29 (31; 33), turn and leave remaining sts. on a spare needle.
Continue on these 29 (31; 33) sts. for first side, dec. 1 st. at neck edge on every row until 22 (24; 26) sts. remain.
Continue straight until front matches back to start of shoulder shaping, ending with right side facing.
Shape shoulder by casting off 8 (8; 8) sts. at beg. of next row, then 7 (8; 9) sts. at beg. of following 2 alternate rows.
With right side facing, slip centre 13 (15; 17) sts. on a spare needle, rejoin appropriate colour to remaining sts., patt. to end. Finish to correspond with first side.

SLEEVES
With No. 10 (3¼ mm) needles and MS, cast on 33 (33; 37) sts. and work 5 cm. (2 in.), k. 1, p. 1 rib, as for back, ending with 1st row.
Next row: Rib 3 (3; 4), m.1, * rib 1, m.1; rep. from * to last 3 (3; 4) sts., rib 3 (3; 4). 61 (61; 67) sts.
Change to No 8 (4 mm) needles and st.st., starting with a k. row, and work straight until sleeve measures 28 (30; 33) cm. 11 (12; 13) in. at centre from start, ending with a p. row. Cast off fairly loosely knitways.

NECK BORDER
Join right shoulder seam.
With right side facing, No. 10 (3¼ mm) needles and MS, start at left shoulder on front and pick up and k. 16 sts. down left side of neck, k. 13 (15; 17) from centre, pick up and k. 16 up right side, then k. 27 (29; 31) from back inc. 4 sts. evenly across 78 (82; 86) sts.
Work 16 rows k. 1, p. 1 rib. Cast off loosely in rib, using a bigger needle.

TO MAKE UP
Do not press. Join left shoulder seam and neck border. Join side seams to markers, then join sleeve seams; insert sleeves.

CHECKERBOARD POLO NECK

MATERIALS

Patons Beehive DK **(MS)**	**50 g. balls**	3	3	3
(L)	**50 g. balls**	1	1	1
(C)	**50 g. balls**	1	1	2

Pair each Nos. 10 (3¼ mm) and 8 (4 mm) needles.

MEASUREMENTS

To fit chest	**cm.**	56	61	66
	in.	22	24	26
Length from top of shoulders	**cm.**	38	42	46
	in.	15	16½	18
Sleeve seam	**cm.**	28	30	33
	in.	11	12	13

TENSION
22 sts. and 30 rows measured over 10 cm. (4 in.) of stocking stitch on No. 8 (4 mm) needles.

ABBREVIATIONS
k., knit; **p.**, purl; **sts.**, stitches; **st.st.**, stocking st.; **mm.**, millimetres; **cm.**, centimetres; **in.**, inches; **m.1**, pick up horizontal loop lying before next st. and work into back of it; **rep.**, repeat; **dec.**, decrease by working 2 sts. together; **inc.**, increase by working into front and back of st.; **beg.**, beginning; **patt.**, pattern; **MS**, Main Shade; **L**, 1st Constrast Shade; **C**, 2nd Contrast Shade.

BACK
**With No. 10 (3¼ mm) needles and MS, cast on 55 (61; 67) sts.
1st row: Right side facing, k. 1, * p. 1, k. 1; rep. from * to end.
2nd row: P. 1, * k. 1, p. 1; rep. from * to end.
Rep. last 2 rows until work measures 45 cm. (2 in.) ending with 1st row.
Next row: Rib 6 (2; 5), m.1, * rib 3 (4; 4), m.1; rep. from * to last 7 (3; 6) sts., rib 7 (3; 6). 70 (76; 82) sts.
Change to No. 8 (4 mm) needles and work in st.st. in checkerboard patt. as follows:
1st row: Right side facing, k. 5 (8; 11) MS, join in L, and k. 12 L, join in 2nd ball MS, and k. 12 MS, join in 2nd ball L and k. 12 L, join in 3rd ball MS and k. 12 MS, join in 3rd ball L and k. 12 L, join in 4th ball MS and k. 5 (8; 1)) MS.
N.B.: Twist yarns on wrong side of work when changing colour to avoid a hole.
2nd row: P. 5 (8; 11) MS, * 12 L, 12 MS; rep. from * to last 17 (20; 23) sts., 12 L, 5 (8; 11) MS.
3rd row: As 2nd, but reading 'k.' for 'p.' throughout.
4th-19th rows: As 2nd and 3rd rows 8 times.
20th row: As 2nd. Break yarns.
21st row: Join in C and k. 5 (8; 11) C, join in MS, and k. 12 MS, join in 2nd ball C and k. 12 C, join in 2nd ball MS and k. 12 MS, join in 3rd ball C and k. 12 C, join in 3rd ball MS and k. 12 MS, join in 4th ball C and k. 5 (8; 11) C.
22nd row: P. 5 (8; 11) C, * 12 MS, 12 C; rep. from * to last 17 (20; 23) sts., 12 MS, 5 (8; 11) C
23rd row: As 22nd, but reading 'k.' for 'p.' throughout.
24th–39th rows: As 22nd and 23rd rows 8 times.
40th row: As 22nd. Break yarns. These 40 rows form patt.
Continue straight in patt. until back measures 23 (27; 29) cm. 9 (10½; 11½) in. at centre from start, ending with a p. row. Place a marker at each end of last row. **
Continue in patt. until back measures 38 (42; 46) cm. 15 (16½; 18) in., ending with right side facing.
Shape shoulders by casting off 8 (8; 8) sts. at beg. of next 2 rows, then 7 (8; 9) sts. at beg. of next 4 rows. Leave remaining 26 (28; 30) sts. on a spare needle.

FRONT
Work as for back from ** to **.
Continue in patt. until front measures 34 (38; 42) cm. 13½ (15; 16½) in. at centre from start, ending with right side facing.
Here divide for neck.
Next row: Patt. 29 (31; 33), turn and leave remaining sts. on a spare needle.
Continue on these 29 (31; 33) sts. for first side, dec. 1 st. at neck edge on every row until 22 (24; 26) sts. remain.
Continue straight until front matches back to start of shoulder shaping, ending with right side facing.
Shape shoulder by casting off 8 (8; 8) sts. at beg. of next row, then 7 (8; 9) sts. at beg. of following 2 alternate rows.
With right side facing, slip centre 12 (14; 16) sts. on a spare needle, rejoin appropriate colour to remaining sts., patt. to end. Finish to correspond with first side.

SLEEVES
With No. 10 (3¼ mm) needles and MS, cast on 33 (33; 37) sts. and work 5 cm. (2 in.), k. 1, p. 1 rib, as for back, ending with 1st row.

Next row: Rib 2 (2; 3), m.1, * rib 1, m.1; rep. from * to last 3 (3; 4) sts., rib 3 (3; 4). 62 (62; 68) sts. Join in MS, change to No. 8 (4 mm) needles and work in patt. as follows:
1st row: Right side facing, k. 13 (13; 16) MS, join in L and k. 12 L, join in 2nd ball MS and k. 12 MS, join in 2nd ball L and k. 12 L, join in 3rd ball MS and k. 13 (13; 16) MS.
Continue in checkboard patt. thus, alternating colours as for back until sleeve measures 28 (30; 33) cm. 11 (12; 13) in. at centre from start, ending with right side facing. Cast off fairly loosely in patt.

NECK BORDER
Join right shoulder seam.
With right side facing, No. 10 (3¼ mm) needles and MS, start at left shoulder on front and pick up and k. 16 sts. down left side of neck, k. 12 (14; 16) from centre inc. 2 sts. evenly pick up and k. 16 up right side, then k. 26 (28; 30) from back inc. 4 sts. evenly across. 76 (80; 84) sts. Work 11 (13; 14) cm. 4½ (5; 5½) in. k. 1, p. 1 rib. Cast off loosely in rib, using a bigger needle.

TO MAKE UP
Do not press. Join left shoulder seam, then join neck border with a flat seam. Join side seams to markers, matching patt. carefully; join sleeve seams; insert sleeves.

CREW NECK WITH STRIPE

MATERIALS

Patons Beehive DK (**MS**)	**50 g. balls**	2	3	3
(**C**)	**50 g. balls**	1	1	1
(**L**)	**50 g. balls**	2	2	2

Pair each Nos. 10 (3¼ mm) and 8 (4 mm) needles.

MEASUREMENTS

To fit chest	**cm.**	56	61	66
	in.	22	24	26
Length from top of shoulders	**cm.**	38	42	46
	in.	15	16½	18
Sleeve seam	**cm.**	28	30	33
	in.	11	12	13

TENSION

22 sts. and 30 rows measured over 10 cm. (4 in.) on No. 8 (4 mm) needles.

ABBREVIATIONS

k., knit; p., purl; **sts.**, stitches; **st.st.**, stocking stitch; **mm.**, millimetres; **cm.**, centimetres; **in.**, inches; **rep.**, repeat; **beg.**, beginning; **dec.**, decrease by working 2 sts. together; **m.1**, pick up horizontal loop lying before next st. and work into back of it; **inc.**, increase by working into front and back of st.; **MS**, Main Shade; **C**, 1st Contrast Shade; **L.**, 2nd Contrast Shade.

BACK

**With No. 10 (3 ¼ mm) needles and MS, cast on 55 (61; 67) sts.
1st row: Right side facing, k. 1, * p. 1, k. 1; rep. from * to end.
2nd row: P. 1, + k. 1, p. 1; rep. from * to end.
Rep last 2 rows until work measures 5 cm. (2 in.), ending with 1st row.
Next row: Rib 5 (8; 3), m.1, * rib 3 (3; 4), m.1; rep. from * to last 5 (8; 4) sts., rib 5 (8; 4). 71 (77; 83) sts.
Change to No. 8 (4 mm) needles and st.st., starting with a k. row, and work straight until back measures 23 (27: 29) cm. 9 (10½; 11½) in. at centre from start, ending with a p. row. Place a marker at each end of last row.
Continue in st.st. in MS until work measures 28 (32; 36) cm. 11 (12½; 14) in. at centre from start, ending with a p. row. Break MS. Join in C and work 4 rows straight. Break C. ** Join in L and continue in st.st. in L until work measures 38 (42; 46) cm. 15 (16½; 18) in., ending with right side facing.
Shape shoulders by casting off 8 (8; 8) sts. at beg. of next 2 rows, then 7 (8; 9) sts. at beg. of next 4 rows. Leave remaining 27 (29; 31) sts. on a spare needle.

FRONT

Work as for back from ** to **.
Join in L and continue in st.st. in L until work measures 34 (38; 42) cm. 13½ (15; 16½) in. at centre from start, ending with right side facing.
Here divide for neck.
Next row: K. 29 (31; 33), turn and leave remaining sts. on a spare needle.
Continue on these 29 (31; 33) sts. for first side, dec. 1 st. at neck edge on every row until 22 (24; 26) sts. remain.
Continue straight until front matches back to start of shoulder shaping, ending with right side facing.
Shape shoulder by casting off 8 (8; 8) sts. at beg. of next row, then 7 (8; 9) sts. at beg. of following 2 alternate rows.
With right side facing, slip centre 13 (15; 17) sts. on a spare needle, rejoin yarn to remaining sts., k. to end. Finish to correspond with first side.

SLEEVES

With No. 10 (3¼ mm) needles and MS, cast on 33 (33; 37) sts. and work 5 cm. (2 in.) k. 1, p. 1 rib, as for back, ending with 1st row.
Next row: Rib 3 (3; 4), m.1, * rib 1, m.1; rep. from * to last 3 (3; 4) sts., rib 3 (3; 4). 61 (61; 67) sts.
Change to No. 8 (4 mm) needles.
Next row: K. 10 (10; 13) MS, join in C and k. 3 C, join in L and k. 35 L, join in 2nd ball C and k. 3 C, join in 2nd ball MS and k. 10 (10; 13) MS.
N.B.: Twist yarns on wrong side of work when changing colour to avoid a hole.
Next row: P. 10 (10; 13) MS, 3 C, 35 L, 3 C, 10 (10; 13) MS.
Next row: K. 10 (10; 13) MS, 3 C, 35 L, 3 C, 10 (10; 13) MS.
The last 2 rows form stripe patt. for sleeves.
Rep. them until sleeve measures 28 (30; 33) cm. 11 (12; 13) in. at centre from start, ending with a p. row. Cast off fairly loosely knitways.

NECK BORDER

Join right shoulder seam.
With right side facing, No. 10 (3¼ mm) needles and L, start at left shoulder on front and pick up and k. 16 sts. down left side of neck, k. 13 (15; 17) from centre inc. 2 sts., pick up and k. 16 up right side, then k. 27 (29; 31) from back inc. 4 sts. evenly across. 78 (82; 86) sts.
Work 16 rows k. 1, p. 1 rib. Cast off loosely in rib, using a bigger needle.

TO MAKE UP

Do not press. Join left shoulder seam, and neck border. Join side seams to markers, then join sleeve seams; insert sleeves matching colours on yoke to sleeve head carefully.

HAT SCARF AND MITTS

MATERIALS

Patons Beehive DK	**Hat**	**50 g. balls**	1
	Scarf	**50 g. balls**	2
	Mitts	**50 g. balls**	1

Pair each Nos. 10 (3¼ mm) and 8 (4 mm) needles.

MEASUREMENTS

Average hat size for 3–7 yr. old.

Scarf Width	**cm.**	15
	in.	6
Length	**cm.**	90
	in.	35½

Mitts
To fit 3–5 (6–8) yrs.

TENSION
22 sts. and 30 rows measured over 10 cm. (4 in.) in stocking stitch on No. 8 (4 mm) needles.

ABBREVIATIONS
k., knit; **p.**, purl; **sts.**, stitches; **st.st.**, stocking stitch; **mm.**, millimetres; **cm.**, centimetres; **in.**, inches; **rep.**, repeat; **dec.**, decrease by working 2 sts. together; **m.1**, pick up horizontal loop lying before next st. and work into back of it; **tog.**, together; **sl.**, slip; **p.s.s.o.**, pass the slipped st. over.

HAT
With No. 10 (3¼ mm) needles, cast on 99 sts. and work 10 cm. (4 in.) k. 1, p. 1 rib.
Change to No. 8 (4 mm) needles and st.st., starting with a k. row and work straight until hat measures 18 cm. (7 in.) at centre from start, ending with a p. row.
Shape crown as follows:
1st row: * K. 9, k. 2 tog.; rep. from * to end. 90 sts.
2nd and every alternate row: P.
3rd row: * K. 8, k. 2 tog.; rep. from * to end. 81 sts.
5th row: * K· 7, k. 2 tog.; rep. from * to end. 72 sts.
7th row: * K. 6, k. 2 tog.; rep. from * to end. 63 sts.
9th row: * K. 5, k. 2 tog.; rep. from * to end. 54 sts.
11th row: * K. 4, k. 2 tog.; rep. from * to end. 45 sts.
13th row: * K. 3, k. 2 tog.; rep. from * to end. 36 sts.
15th row: * K. 2, k. 2 tog.; rep. from * to end. 27 sts.
17th row: * K. 1, k. 2 tog.; rep. from * to end. 18 sts.
19th row: * K. 2 tog.; rep. from * to end. 9 sts.
20th row: P.
Break yarn. Thread through remaining sts., draw up tightly and fasten off.

SCARF
With No. 8 (4 mm) needles, cast on 39 sts.
1st row: Right side facing k. 3, * p. 1, k. 1; rep. from * to last 2 sts., k. 2.
2nd row: K.2, * p.1, k. 1; rep. from * to last st., k.1.
Rep. last 2 rows until work measures 90 cm. (35½ in.). Cast off evenly in rib.

MITTS
With No. 10 (3¼ mm) needles, cast on 33 (37) sts. and work 18 (20) rows k. 1, p. 1 rib.
Change to No. 8 (4 mm) neeedles and starting with a k. row, work 4 rows st.st.
Increase for thumb as follows:
1st row: K. 16 (18), m.1, k. 1, m.1, k. 16 (18).
2nd and every alternate row: P.
3rd row: K. 16 (18), m.1, k. 3, m.1, k. 16 (18).
5th row: K. 16 (18), m.1, k. 5, m.1, k. 16 (18).
Continue increasing 2 sts., thus on every alternate row until there are 43 (49) sts.
Next row: P.
Divide for thumb as follows:
Next row: K. 27 (31), turn.
Next row: P. 11 (13), turn. Work 10 (14) rows straight on these 11 (13) sts.
Next row: K. 1, * k. 2 tog.; rep. from * to end. 6 (7) sts.
Next row: P. 2 (1), (p. 2 tog.) 2 (3) times. 4 (4) sts.
Break yarn. Thread through remaining sts., draw up tightly and fasten off. Join thumb seam.
With right side facing rejoin yarn at base of seam and pick up and k. 1 st. from thumb, then k. remaining 16 (18) sts. 33 (37) sts.
Starting with a p. row, work 15 (19) rows straight in st.st. over all sts.
Next row: K. 1, (sl. 1, k. 1, p.s.s.o., k. 11 [13], k. 2 tog., k. 1) twice.
Next row: P.
Next row: K. 1, (sl. 1, k. 1, p.s.s.o., k. 9 [11], k. 2 tog., until 13 (17) sts. remain. Cast off. Make another mitt the same.

TO MAKE UP
Hat
Join centre back seam. If desired, make a pom-pom, attach to a twisted cord and sew to top. Turn back brim as illustrated.
Scarf
Cut 20 cm. (8 in.) lengths of yarn. Using 6 strands together each time, double yarn and knot along short ends of scarf as illustrated. Trim fringes.
Mitts
Join seam.

FAIR ISLE CREW NECK

MATERIALS

Patons Beehive DK **(MS)**	**50 g. balls**	2	2	2
(A)	**50 g. balls**	1	1	2
(B)	**50 g. balls**	1	1	1
(C)	**50 g. balls**	1	1	1
(D)	**50 g. balls**	1	1	1

Pair each Nos. 10 (3¼ mm) and 8 (4 mm) needles.

MEASUREMENTS

To fit chest	**cm.**	56	61	66
	in.	22	24	26
Length from top of shoulders	**cm.**	38	42	46
	in.	15	16½	18
Sleeve seam	**cm.**	28	30	33
	in.	11	12	13

TENSION
26 sts. and 26 rows measured over 10 cm. (4 in.) of 5 colour pattern on No. 8 (4 mm) needles.

ABBREVIATIONS
k., knit; **p.**, purl; **sts.**, stitches; **mm.**, millimetres; **cm.**, centimetres; **in.**, inches; **rep.**, repeat; **dec.**, decrease by working 2 sts. together; **beg.**, beginning; **patt.**, pattern; **m.1**, pick up horizontal loop lying before next st. and work into back of it; **tog.**, together; **sl.**, slip; **p.s.s.o.**, pass the slipped st. over; **MS**, Main Shade; **A**, 1st Contrast Shade; **B**, 2nd Contrast Shade; **C**, 3rd Contrast Shade; **D**, 4th Contrast Shade.

N.B.: When working 5 colour patt. from chart, strand yarns loosely across at back of work over not more than 3 sts. at a time to keep fabric elastic, twisting yarns on wrong side of work when changing colour to avoid a hole

BACK
**With No. 10 (3¼ mm) needles and MS, cast on 55 (61; 67) sts.
1st row: Right side facing, k. 1, * p. 1, k. 1; rep. from * to end.
2nd row: P. 1, * k. 1, p. 1; rep. from * to end.
Rep. last 2 rows until work measures 5 cm. (2 in.), ending with 1st row.
Next row: Rib 2 (3; 4), m.1, * rib 2, m.1; rep. from * to last 3 (4; 5) sts., rib 3 (4; 5). 81 (89; 97) sts.
Join in A, change to No. 8 (4 mm) needles and work in patt. from chart, rep. the 8 patt. sts. 10 (11; 12) times across and last st. on k. rows and 1st st. on p. rows as indicated.
Read odd rows k., from right to left and even rows p. from left to right.
Work straight in patt. until back measures 23 (27; 29) cm. 9 (10½; 11½) in. at centre from start, ending with right side facing. Place a marker at each end of last row. **
Continue straight in patt. until back measures 38 (42; 46) cm. 15 (16½; 18) in. at centre from start, ending with right side facing.
Shape shoulders by casting off 8 (9; 10) sts. at beg. of next 6 rows. Leave remaining 33 (35; 37) sts. on a spare needle.

FRONT
Work as for back from ** to **.
Work straight until front measures 34 (38; 42) cm. 13½ (15; 16½) in. at centre from start, ending with right sides facing.
Here divide for neck.
Next row: Patt. 31 (34; 37), turn and leave remaining sts. on a spare needle.
Continue on these 31 (34; 37) sts. for first side, dec. 1 st. at neck edge on every row until 24 (27; 30) sts. remain.
Continue straight until front matches back at armhole edge, ending with right side facing.
Shape shoulder by casting off 8 (9; 10) sts. at beg. of next and following 2 alternate rows.
With right side facing, slip centre 19 (21; 23) sts. on a spare needle, rejoin appropriate colours to remaining sts., patt. to end. Finish to correspond with first side.

SLEEVES
With No. 10 (3¼ mm) needles and MS, cast on 33 (33; 37) sts. and work 5 cm. (2 in.) k. 1, p. 1 rib as for back, ending with 1st row.
Continue as follows:
1st and 2nd sizes only:
Next row: Rib 3 (3), m.1, * rib 1, m.1, work into front and back of next st., m.1; rep. from * to last 4 (4) sts., rib 4 (4). 73 (73) sts.
3rd size only:
Next row: Rib 4, m.1, * rib 1, m.1, work into front and back of next st., m.1; rep. from * to last 5 sts., work into front and back of next st., rib 4. 81 sts.
All sizes:
Change to No. 8 (4 mm) needles and starting with a 1st row, work straight in patt. as for back, repeating the 8 patt. sts. 9 (9; 10) times across until sleeve measures 28 (30; 33) cm. 11 (12; 13) in. at centre from start, ending with right side facing. Cast off fairly loosely in patt.

NECK BORDER
Join right shoulder seam.
With right side facing, No. 10 (3¼ mm) needles and MS, start at left shoulder on front and pick up and knit 15 sts. down left side of neck, k. 19 (21; 23) from centre, pick up and knit 15 up right side, then k. 33 (35; 37) from back. 82 (86; 90) sts.
Work 16 rows k. 1, p. 1 rib. Cast off loosely in rib, using a bigger needle.

TO MAKE UP
Do not press. Join left shoulder seam, then join neck border with a flat seam. Join side and sleeve seams, matching patt. carefully, insert sleeves.
Fold neck border in half to wrong side and slip-hem loosely in position.

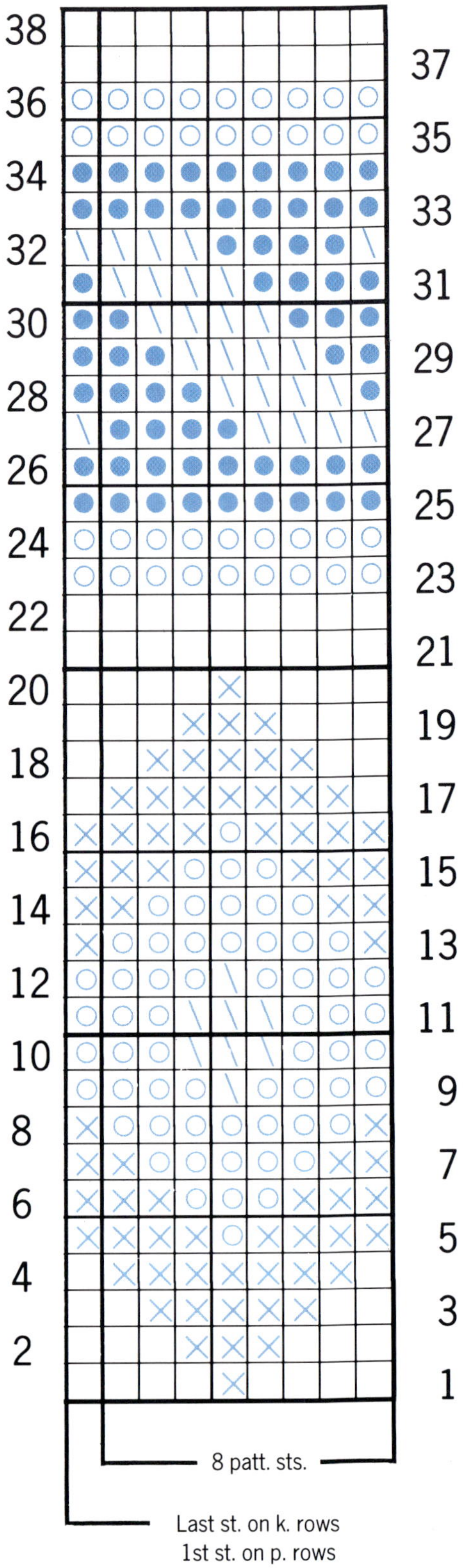

KEY
□ = Main Shade **MS**
× = 1st Contrast Shade **A**
○ = 2nd Contrast Shade **B**
/ = 3rd Contrast Shade **C**
● = 4th Contrast Shade **D**

Denis Lawson and Diane Fletcher

JACKET TRIO

Star of Bill Forsyth's haunting Scottish comedy *Local Hero*, Denis Lawson will be remembered by hundreds of thousands for his glorious miming talent (used to devastating effect in the West End hit musical *Mr Cinders*). Diane Fletcher stirred audiences to rueful laughter in the West End hit *Why Me* opposite Richard Briers. Work may keep them apart, but years of devotion and their small son Jamie, keep Diane and Denis together.

MAN'S JACKET

MATERIALS

Patons Moorland Shetland DK	**50 g. balls**	11	12	12	13

Pair each Nos. 8 (4 mm) and 10 (3¼ mm) needles.
2 stitch holders. 10 buttons.

MEASUREMENTS

To fit chest	**cm.**	91	97	102	107
	in.	36	38	40	42
Length from top of shoulders	**cm.**	72	74	74	75
	in.	28½	29	29	29½
Sleeve seam, cuff turned back	**cm.**	46	47	47	48
	in.	18	18½	18½	19

TENSION
Pattern is based on a standard stocking stitch tension of 22 sts. and 30 rows measured over 10 cm. (4 in.) on No. 8 (4 mm) needles.

ABBREVIATIONS
k., knit; **p.**, purl; **sts.**, stitches; **st.st.**, stocking st.; **mm.**, millimetres; **cm.**, centimetres; **in.**, inches; **rep.**, repeat; **beg.**, beginning; **patt.**, pattern; **dec.**, decrease by working 2 sts. together; **inc.**, increase by working into front and back of st.

BACK
With No. 10 (3¼ mm) needles, cast on 119 (125; 131; 137) sts.
1st row: Right side facing, p. 5, * k. 1, p. 5; rep. from * to end.
2nd row: K. 5, * p. 1, k. 5; rep. from * to end.
These 2 rows from patt. Work straight in patt. until work measures 4 cm. (1½ in.), then change to No. 8 (4 mm) needles and continue in patt. until back measures 51 cm. (20 in.) at centre from start, ending with 2nd row.
Continue in patt., shaping armholes by casting off 3 sts. at beg. of next 2 rows, then dec. 1 st. at each end of next and every alternate row until 85 (89; 93; 97) sts. remain.
Work straight until back measures 72 (74; 74; 75) cm. 28½ (29; 29; 29½) in. at centre from start, ending with right side facing.
Shape shoulders by casting off 7 (8; 9; 8) sts. at beg. of next 2 rows, then 8 (8; 8; 9) sts. at beg. of next 4 rows. Cast off remaining 39 (41; 43; 45) sts.

POCKET LININGS
With No. 8 (4 mm) needles, cast on 31 sts. and work 13 cm. (5 in.) st.st., ending with a p. row, and inc. 1 st. at each end of last row. 33 sts.
Leave sts. on a spare needle and make another one the same.

LEFT FRONT
With No. 10 (3¼ mm) needles, cast on 58 (61; 64; 67) sts.
1st row: Right side facing, * p. 5, k. 1; rep. from * to last 4 (1; 4; 1) sts. p. 4 (1; 4; 1).
2nd row: K. 4 (1; 4; 1), * p. 1, k. 5; rep. from * to end. These 2 rows form patt. for left front.
Rep. them until work measures 4 cm. (1½ in.) at centre from start, then change to No. 8 (4 mm) needles and continue in patt. until front measures 16 cm. (6½ in.) at centre from start, ending with right side facing. Place pocket lining as follows:
Next row: Patt. 10 (10; 10; 16).
Slip next 33 sts. on a stitch-holder and in place of these patt. across sts. of one pocket lining, patt. 15 (18; 21; 18).
Continue straight in patt. until front matches back at side edge, ending with right side facing.
Shape armhole by casting off 3 sts. at beg. of next row, work 1 row straight, then dec. 1 st. at beg., of next and every alternate row until 41 (43; 45; 47) sts. remain.
Work straight until front measures 65 (66; 66; 67) cm. 25½ (26; 26; 26½) in. at centre from start, ending with wrong side facing.
Shape neck by casting off 8 (9; 10; 11) sts. at beg of next row, then dec. 1 st. at neck edge on every row until 23 (24; 25; 26) sts. remain.
Work straight until front matches back at armhole edge, ending with right side facing.
Shape shoulder by casting off 7 (8; 9; 9) sts. at beg. of next row, then 8 (8; 8; 9) sts. at beg. of following 2 alternate rows.

RIGHT FRONT
With No. 10 (3¼ mm) needles, cast on 58 (61; 64; 67) sts.
1st row: Right side facing, p. 4 (1; 4; 1), * k. 1, p. 5; rep. from * to end.
2nd row: * K. 5, p. 1; rep. from * to last 4 (1; 4; 1) sts., k. 4 (1; 4; 1). Rep. last 2 rows until work measures 4 cm. (1½ in.), then change to No. 8 (4 mm) needles and continue in patt. until work measures 16 cm. (6½ in.) at centre from start, ending with right side facing.
Place pocket lining as follows:
Next row: Patt. 15 (18; 21; 18), slip next 33 sts. on a stitch-holder and in place of these patt. across sts. of 2nd pocket lining, patt. 10 (10; 10; 16).
Finish to correspond with left front, reversing all shapings.

SLEEVES
With No. 10 (3¼ mm) needles, cast on 53 (59; 59; 65) sts. and starting with 1st row, work 13 cm. (5 in.) rib patt. as for back.
Change to No. 8 (4 mm) needles and continue in patt. shaping sides by inc. 1 st. at each end of 9th and every following 6th row until there are 83 (89; 89; 95) sts., taking inc. sts. into patt.
Work straight until sleeve seam measures 52 (53; 53; 54) cm. 20½ (21; 21; 21½) in., ending with right side facing.
Shape top by casting off 3 sts. at beg. of next 2 rows, then dec. 1 st. at each end of next and every alternate row until 41 (45; 45; 49) sts.
Work 1 row straight, then dec. 1 st. at each end of every row until 21 sts. remain, all sizes. Cast off.

FRONT BORDERS
Right: With No. 10 (3¼ mm) needles, cast on 11 sts.
1st row: Right side facing, k. 2, * p. 1, k. 1; rep. from * to last st., k. 1.
2nd row: K. 1, * p. 1, k. 1; rep. from * to end.
Rep. last 2 rows until border fits up right front to start of neck shaping, ending with right side facing.
For a good fit, sew border in position as you go along, stretching slightly to prevent fluting and when it measures required length, cast off evenly in rib.
Left: Work to correspond with right border with the addition of 10 buttonholes. 1st to come 2 cm. (1 in.) above start of border, 10th 1 cm. (½ in.) below start of neck shaping and remainder spaced evenly.
First mark position of buttons on right border with pins to ensure even spacing and then work and then work holes to correspond.
To make a buttonhole:
Right side facing, rib 4, cast off 3, rib to end.
Work back in rib, casting on 3 over those cast off.

POCKET TOPS
With right side facing, No. 10 (3¼ mm) needles and starting with 1st row, work 7 rows k. 1, p. 1 rib as for front border, across each set of 33 pocket sts., cast off evenly in rib.

COLLAR
With No. 10 (3¼ mm) needles, cast on 125 (129; 129; 133) sts. and starting with 1st row, work straight in k. 1, p. 1 rib as for front border until collar measures 10 cm. (4 in.) from start.
Continue in rib, shaping collar by casting off in rib, 4 sts. at beg. of every row until 53 (57; 57; 61) sts. remain. Cast off in rib.

TO MAKE UP
Join shoulder, side and sleeve seams; insert sleeves. Pin cast-off edge of collar round neck, starting and ending in centre of front borders; sew in position. Catch down sides of pocket tops neatly to main work, then sew linings lightly in position on wrong side. Sew on buttons.

WOMAN'S JACKET

MATERIALS

Patons Promise	**40 g. balls**	11	12	12	13

Pair each Nos. 8 (4 mm) and 10 (3¼ mm) needles. 9 buttons.

MEASUREMENTS

To fit bust	**cm.**	81	86	91	97
	in.	32	34	36	38
Length from top of shoulders	**cm.**	82	84	84	85
	in.	32½	33	33	33½
Sleeve seam, all sizes	**cm.**	43	43	43	43
	in.	17	17	17	17

TENSION
Pattern is based on a standard stocking stitch tension of 22 sts. and 30 rows measured over 10 cm. (4 in.) on No. 8 (4 mm) needles.

ABBREVIATIONS
k., knit; **p.**, purl, **sts.**, stitches; **st.st.**, stocking st.; **mm.**, millimetres; **cm.**, centimetres; **in.**, inches; **rep.**, repeat; **beg.**, beginning; **patt.**, pattern; **dec.**, decrease by working 2 sts. together; **inc.**, increase by working into front and back of st.; **m.1**, pick up horizontal loop lying before next st. and work into back of it; **tog.**, together; **t.b.l.**, through back of loops.

LEFT FRONT
With No. 8 (4 mm) needles, cast on 64 (68; 71; 75) sts.
1st row: Right side facing, * p. 6, k. 1; rep. from * to last 1 (5; 1; 5) sts., p. 1 (5; 1; 5).
2nd row: K. 1 (5; 1; 5), * p.1, k. 6; rep. from * to end.
Rep. last 2 rows until work measures 21 cm. (8 ½ in.) at centre from start, ending with 1st row.
Shape as follows:
Next row: K. 1 (5; 1; 5), * p. 1, k. 4, k. 2 tog.; rep. from * to end. 55 (59; 61; 65) sts.
Continue in patt. as follows:
1st row: * p. 5, k. 1; rep. from * to last 1 (5; 1; 5) sts., p. 1 (5; 1; 5).
2nd row: K. 1 (5; 1; 5), * p. 1, k. 5; rep. from * to end.
Rep. last 2 rows until work measures 42 cm. (16½ in.) at centre from start, ending with 1st row.
Continue as follows:
1st and 3rd sizes only
Next row: K. 1, * p. 1, k. 2 tog. t.b.l., k. 3; rep. from * to end. 46 (51) sts.
2nd and 4th sizes only
Next row: K. 2 tog. t.b.l., k. 3, * p. 1, k. 2 tog t.b.l., k. 3; rep. from * to end. 49 (54) sts.
All sizes
Continue in patt. as follows:
1st row: * p. 4, k. 1; rep. from * to last 1 (4; 1; 4) sts., p. 1 (4; 1; 4).
2nd row: K. 1 (4; 1; 4), * p. 1, k. 4; rep. from * to end.
Rep. last 2 rows until work measures 57 cm. (22½ in.) at centre from start, ending with right side facing.
Start to shape front edge by dec. 1 st. at end of next and every following 4th row until 42 (45; 47; 50) sts. remain. Work 3 rows straight.
Continue shaping front edge and at the same time shape armhole as follows:
Next row: Cast off 3, patt. to last 2 sts., work 2 tog.
Work 1 row straight.
Now dec. 1 st. at armhole edge on next and every alternate row and at the same time continue dec. 1 st. at front edge on every 4th row from last dec. until 28 (29; 30; 31) sts. remain.
Now keep armhole edge straight and continue dec. 1 st. at front edge on every following 6th row from last dec. until 22 (23; 24; 25) sts. remain.
Work straight until front measures 82 (84; 84; 85) cm. 32½ (33; 33; 33½) in. at centre from start, ending with right side facing.
Shape shoulder by casting off 8 (7; 8; 9) sts. at beg. of next row, then 7 (8; 8; 8) sts. at beg. of following 2 alternate rows.

RIGHT FRONT
With No. 8 (4 mm) needles, cast on 64 (68; 71; 75) sts.
1st row: Right side facing, p. 1 (5; 1; 5), * k. 1, p. 6; rep. from * to end.
2nd row: * k. 6, p. 1; rep. from * to last 1 (5; 1; 5) sts., k. 1 (5; 1; 5).
Finish to correspond with left front, reversing all shapings.

BACK
With No. 8 (4 mm) needles, cast on 132 (139; 146; 153) sts.
1st row: Right side facing, p. 6 * k. 1, p. 6; rep. from * to end.
2nd row: K. 6, * p. 1, k. 6; rep. from * to end.
Rep. last 2 rows until work measures 21 cm. (8½ in.) at centre from start, ending with 1st row.
Shape as follows:
Next row: K. 4, k. 2 tog., * p. 1, k. 4, k. 2 tog.; rep. from * to end. 113 (119; 125; 131) sts.
Continue in patt. as follows:
1st row: P. 5, * k. 1, p. 5; rep. from * to end.
2nd row: K. 5, * p. 1, k. 5; rep. from * to end.
Rep. last 2 rows until work measures 42 cm. (16½ in.) at centre from start, ending with 1st row.
Next row: K. 2 tog. t.b.l., k. 3, * p. 1, k. 2 tog. t.b.l., k. 3; rep. from * to end. 94 (99; 104; 109) sts.
Continue in patt. as follows:
1st row: P. 4, * k. 1, p. 4; rep. from * to end.
2nd row: K. 4, * p. 1, k. 4; rep. from * to end.
These last 2 rows form main rib patt. for bodice and sleeves.
Work straight in patt. until back matches front at side edge, ending with right side facing.
Shape armholes by casting off 3 sts. at beg. of next 2 rows, then dec. 1 st. at each end of next and every alternate row until 74 (77; 80; 83) sts. remain.
Keeping continuity of rib, work straight until back matches front at armhole edge, ending with right side facing.
Shape shoulders by casting off 8 (7; 8; 9) sts. at beg. of next 2 rows, then 7 (8; 8; 8) sts. at beg. of next 4 rows. Cast off remaining 30 (31; 32; 33) sts.

SLEEVES
With No. 10 (3¼ mm) needles, cast on 44 (48; 48; 52) sts. and work 7 cm. (3 in.) k. 1, p. 1 rib.
Next row: Rib 5 (6; 6; 8), m.1, * rib 1, m.1; rep. from * to last 5 (7; 7; 8) sts., rib 5 (7; 7; 8). 79 (84; 84; 89) sts.
Change to No. 8 (4 mm) needles and rib patt. as follows:
1st row: Right side facing, p. 4, * k. 1, p. 4; rep. from * to end.
2nd row: K. 4, *p. 1, k. 4; rep. from * to end.
Rep. last 2 rows until sleeve measures 43 cm. (17 in.) at centre from start, ending with right side facing.
Shape top by casting off 3 sts. at beg. of next 2 rows, then dec. 1 st. at each end of next and every alternate row until 37 (38; 38; 39) sts remain.
Work 1 row straight, then dec. 1 st. at each end of every row until 21 (22; 22; 23) sts. remain.
Cast off.

FRONT BORDER
Join shoulder seams.
With No. 10 (3¼ mm) needles, cast on 13 sts.
1st row: Right side facing, k. 2, * p. 1 , k. 1; rep. from * to last st., k. 1.
2nd row: K. 1, * p. 1, k. 1; rep. from * to end.
Rep. last 2 rows 5 times more.
Make 1st buttonhole in next 2 rows as follows:
Rib 5, cast off 3, rib to end; work back in rib, casting on 3 over those cast off.
Continue in rib, making a further 8 buttonholes at 6 cm. (2½ in.) intervals, then work straight until border fits up right front, round neck and down left front.
For a good fit, sew border in postion as you go along, stretching slightly to prevent fluting and when it measures required length, cast off evenly in rib.

TO MAKE UP
Do not press.
Join side and sleeve seams; insert sleeves, easing in excess fullness at top of sleeve head.
Sew on buttons.

BOY'S JACKET

MATERIALS				
Patons Beehive DK (**MS**) and oddments of 5 contrasting shades for man and balloons	**50 g. balls**	4	5	5
Pair each Nos. 10 (3¼ mm) and 8 (4 mm) needles.				
Buttons		7	7	8
MEASUREMENTS				
To fit chest	**cm.**	61	66	71
	in.	24	26	28
Length from top of shoulders	**cm.**	43	47	51
	in.	17	18½	20
Sleeve seam	**cm.**	30	33	36
	in.	12	13	14

TENSION
Pattern is based on a standard stocking stitch tension of 22 sts. and 30 rows measured over 10 cm. (4 in.) on No. 8 (4 mm) needles.

ABBREVIATIONS
k., knit; **p.**, purl; **sts.**, stitches; **st.st.**, stocking st.; **mm.**, millimetres; **cm.**, centimetres; **in.**, inches; **rep.**, repeat; **beg.**, beginning; **patt.**, pattern; **dec.**, decrease by working 2 sts. together; **inc.**, increase by working into front and back of st.; **m.1**, pick up horizontal loop lying before next st. and work into back of it; **tog.**, together; **t.b.l.**, through back of loops; **MS.**, Main Shade.

BACK
With No. 10 (3¼ mm) needles and MS., cast on 61 (67; 73) sts.
1st row: Right side facing, k. 1, * p. 1, k. 1; rep. from * to end.
2nd row: P. 1, * k. 1, p. 1; rep. from * to end.
Rep. last 2 rows until work measures 5 cm. (2 in.), ending with 1st row.
Next row: Rib 5 (8; 2), m.1, * rib 3 (3; 4) m.1; rep. from * to last 5 (8; 3) sts., rib 5 (8; 3). 79 (85; 91) sts.
Change to No. 8 (4 mm) needles and st.st., starting with a k. row and work 4 (10; 16) rows straight.
Joining in and breaking off colours as required, work in patt. from chart, reading odd rows k. from right to left and even rows p. from left to right.
N.B.: Twist yarns on wrong side of work when changing colour to avoid a hole.
Work straight in patt. until back measures 28 (30; 34) cm. 11 (12; 13½) in. at centre from start, ending with a p. row. Place a marker at each end of last row.
Continue working in patt. from chart until the 99 rows are done, then work straight in st.st. in MS. until back measures 43 (47; 51) cm. 17 (18½; 20) in. at centre from start, ending with a p. row.
Shape shoulders by casting off 9 (9; 11) sts. at beg. of next 2 rows, then 9 (10; 10) sts. at beg. of next 4 rows.
Leave remaining 25 (27; 29) sts. on a spare needle.

LEFT FRONT
**With No. 10 (3¼ mm) needles and MS, cast on 29 (31; 35) sts. and work 5 cm. (2 in.) k. 1 p. 1 rib, as for back, ending with 1st row.
Next row: Rib 2 (2; 1), m.1, * rib 3 (3; 4) m.1; rep. from * to last 3 (2; 2) sts., rib 3 (2; 2). 38 (41; 44) sts.
Change to No. 8 (4 mm) needles and st.st., starting with a k. row, and work 2 rows straight. **
Divide for pocket as follows:
Next row: K. 12 (13; 14), turn and leave remaining

sts. on a spare needle.
Continue on these 12 (13; 14) sts. as follows: Cast on 20 sts. for pocket lining, p. across these sts., p. 12 (13; 14). 32 (33; 34) sts.
Work 23 (25; 27) rows straight.
Next row: Cast off 20, p. to end. 12 (13; 14) sts. Leave sts. on a spare needle.
With right side facing, rejoin yarn to 26 (28; 30) sts. on spare needle, and work 26 (28; 30) rows straight. Leave sts. on a spare needle.
With right side facing, return to 12 (13; 14) sts. at side edge and k. across, then k. across remaining 26 (28; 30) sts. 38 (41; 44) sts.
Work straight until front matches back at side edge, ending with right side facing. Place a marker at end of last row, then continue until front measures 39 (43; 47) cm. 15½ (17; 18½) in. at centre from start, ending with wrong side facing.
Shape neck by casting off 5 (6; 7) sts. at beg. of next row, then dec. 1 st. at neck edge on every row until 27 (29; 31) sts. remain.
Work a few rows straight until front matches back to start of shoulder shaping, ending with right side facing.
Shape shoulder by casting off 9 (9; 11) sts. at beg. of next row, then 9 (10; 10) sts. at beg. of following 2 alternate rows.

RIGHT FRONT
Work as for left front from ** to **.
Divide for pocket as follows:
Next row: K. 26 (28; 30), turn and leave remaining sts. on a spare needle.
Continue on these 26 (28; 30) sts. and work 25 (27; 29) rows straight. Leave sts. on a spare needle.
With right side facing, rejoin yarn to remaining 12 (13; 14) sts., cast on 20 sts. for pocket lining, k. across these sts., k. to end. 32 (33; 34) sts.
Work 23 (25; 27) rows straight.
Next row: Cast off 20 sts., k. to end.
Next row: P. Leave sts. on a spare needle.
With right side facing, return to 26 (28; 30) sts. at front edge and k. across, then k. across remaining 12 (13; 14) sts. 38 (41; 44) sts.
Finish to correspond with left front, reversing all shapings.

SLEEVES
With No. 10 (3¼ mm) needles and MS., cast on 33 (37; 37) sts. and work 5 cm. (2 in.) k. 1, p. 1 rib, as for back, ending with 1st row.
Next row: Rib 3 (4; 4), m.1, * rib 1, m.1; rep. from * to last 3 (4; 4) sts., rib 3 (4; 4). 61 (67; 67) sts.
Change to No. 8 (4 mm) needles and stocking-stitch, starting with a k. row, and work straight until sleeve measures 30 (33; 36) cm., 12 (13; 14) in. at centre from start, ending with a p. row.
Cast off loosely knitways.

FRONT BORDERS
Right: With No. 10 (3¼ mm) needles and MS, cast on 9 sts.
1st row: Right side facing, k. 2, * p. 1, k. 1; rep. from * to last st., k. 1.
2nd row: K. 1, * p. 1, k. 1; rep. from * to end.
Rep. last 2 rows until border fits up right front to start of neck shaping, ending with right side facing.

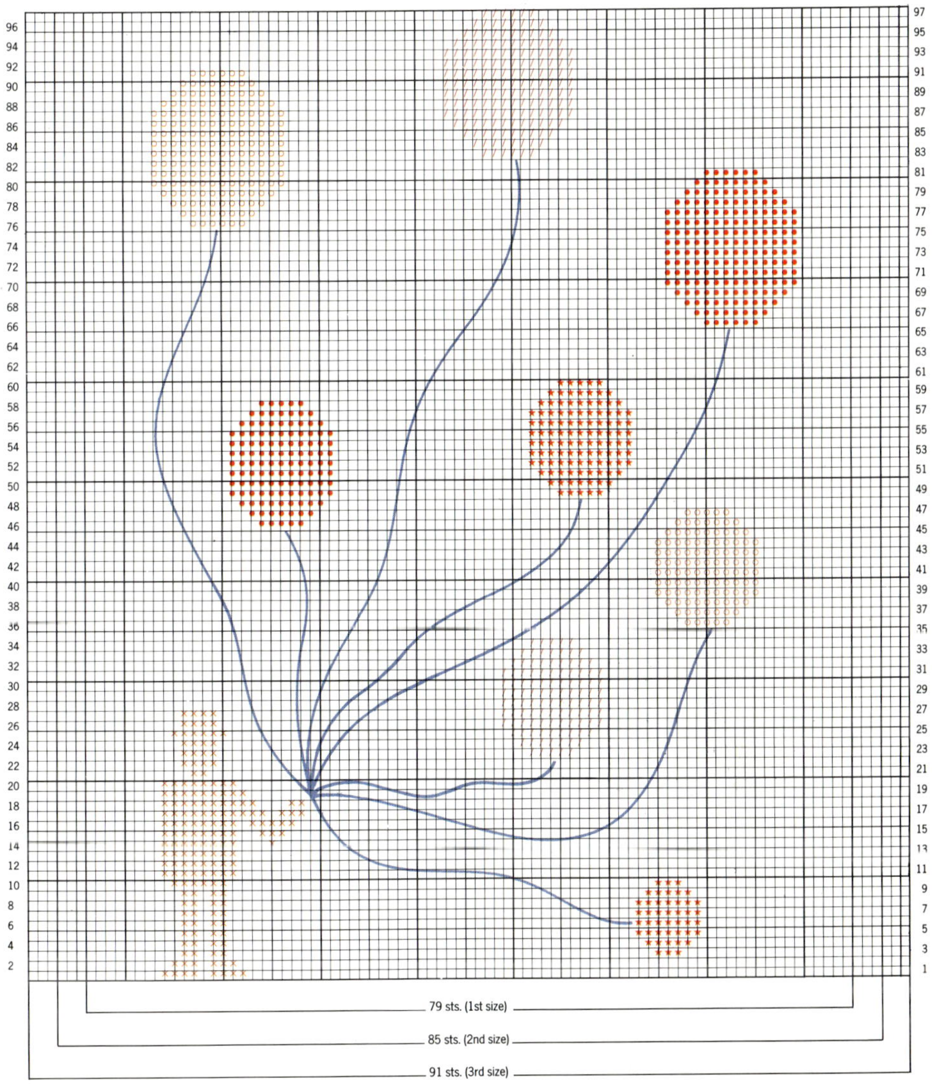

KEY □ = Main Shade ○ = Gold / = Red × = Cream ● = Turquoise ★ = Green

For a good fit, sew border in position as you go along, stretching slightly to prevent fluting and when it measures required length, leave sts. on a safety-pin at top.
Left: Work to correspond with right border with the addition of 6 (6; 7) buttonholes. 1st to come 2 cm. (1 in.) above start of border, 6th (6th; 7th) 4 cm. (1½ in.) below start of neck shaping and remainder spaced evenly.
First mark position of buttons on right border with pins to ensure even spacing, then work holes to correspond.
To make a buttonhole:
Right side facing, rib 3, cast off 3, rib to end; work back in rib, casting on 3 over those cast off.

NECK BORDER
With right side facing, No. 10 (3¼ mm) needles and MS., rib 9 from right border, pick up and k. 19 (20; 21) sts. up right side of neck, k. 25 (27; 29) from back, pick up and k. 19 (20; 21) down left side, then rib 9 from left border. 81 (85; 89) sts.
Starting with 2nd row, work 3 rows rib, as for front border. Make a buttonhole in next 2 rows, then work 6 rows rib. Make a buttonhole in next 2 rows, then work 2 rows rib. Cast off evenly in rib.

POCKET BORDERS
With right side facing, No. 10 (3¼ mm) needles and MS., pick up and k. 23 (25; 27) sts. along pocket edge and starting with 2nd row, work 5 rows k. 1, p. 1 rib, as for front border. Cast off evenly in rib.

TO MAKE UP
Do not press. Join shoulder and sleeve seams, then join side seams to markers; insert sleeves. Catch down short ends of pocket borders neatly to main work, then sew linings lightly in position on wrong side.
Sew on buttons. Using white yarn and chain stitch, embroider 'strings' of balloons as illustrated.

Jilly Johnson

MOTHER AND DAUGHTER MINI WITH STRIPED LEG WARMERS

Jilly Johnson, one time Page Three Girl, now a top model with her own lingerie business, makes the most of legs that have already made her a fortune in our mini sweater dress and leg warmers. A mini version of mother's mini looks just as becoming on daughter, Lucy.

MATERIALS

Dress				
Patons Beehive DK, Main Shade **(M)**	**50 g. balls**	7	9	11
1st Contrast **(A)**	**50 g. balls**	2	3	4
2nd Contrast **(B)**	**50 g. balls**	2	3	4
3rd Contrast **(C)**	**50 g. balls**	1	2	2
Leg Warmers				
Patons Beehive DK, **(M)**	**50 g. balls**	1	1	1
(A)	**50 g. balls**	1	1	1
(B)	**50 g. balls**	1	1	1
(C)	**50 g. balls**	1	1	1

Pair Milward needles each Nos. 8 (4 mm) and 10 (3¼ mm).

MEASUREMENTS

To fit bust	**cm.**	66-71	76-81	86-91
	in.	26-28	30-32	34-36
Actual width all round, approximately	**cm.**	86	99	112
	in.	34	39	44
Length	**cm.**	61	74	86
	in.	24	29	34
Sleeve seam	**cm.**	36	41	44
	in.	14	16	17½
Leg Warmers, length when worn, approximately	**cm.**	25	28	30
	in.	10	11	12

TENSION
14 sts. in width to 5 cm. (2 in.) measured over patt. not stretched, using No. 8 (4mm) needles.

ABBREVIATIONS
k., knit; **p.**, purl; **sts.** stitches; **patt.**, pattern; **inc.**, increase, increasing; **dec.**, decrease, decreasing; **beg.**, beginning; **alt.**, alternate; **rep.** repeat; **cm.**, centimetres; **in.**, inches.

DRESS
Front
With No. 10 (3¼ mm) needles and M, cast on 72 (84; 100) sts.
1st row: (right side): K. 3, (p. 2, k. 2) to last st., k1.
2nd row: K. 1, (p. 2, k. 2) to last 3 sts., p. 2, k. 1.
Rep. these 2 rows for 15 (17; 18) cm., 6 (6½; 7) in., ending after a 1st row.
Next row: Rib 1 (3; 9), (inc. once in each of next 2 sts., rib 1) 23 (26; 27) times, rib to end. 118 (136; 154) sts.
Change to No. 8 (4 mm) needles and patt. thus:–
(**N.B.**: Use a separate ball of yarn for each colour area, twisting yarns on wrong side when changing colours to avoid a hole).
1st row: K., (10M, 8A) to last 10 sts., 10M.
2nd row: In M, k. 9, p. 1, (p. 1A, k. 2A, p. 2A, k. 2A, p. 1A, p. 1M, k. 8M, p. 1M) to end, but ending last repeat p. 1M, k. 9M.
3rd row: In M, p. 9, k. 1, (k. 1A, p. 2A, k. 2A, p. 2A, k. 1A, k. 1M, p. 8M, k. 1M) to end, but ending last repeat k. 1M, p. 9M.
4th row: As 2nd.
5th row: K. 10M, (k. 1A, p. 2A, k. 2A, p. 2A, k. 1A, k. 10M) to end.
6th row: P. 10M, (p. 1A, k. 2A, p. 2A, k. 2A, p. 1A, p. 10M) to end.
7th row: As 5th.
8th and 9th rows: As 2nd and 3rd.
10th row: As 2nd.
11th row: K., 9B, (10M, 8B) to last st., 1B.
12th row: (P. 2B, k. 2B) twice, p. 1B, (p. 1M, k. 8M, p. 1M, p. 1B, k. 2B, p. 2B, k. 2B, p. 1B) to end, but ending last repeat k. 2B, p. 2B.
13th row: (K. 2B, p. 2B) twice, k. 1B, (k. 1M, p. 8M, k. 1M, k. 1B, p. 2B, k. 2B, p. 2B, k. 1B) to end but ending last repeat p. 2B, k. 2B.
14th row: As 12th.
15th row: (K. 2B, p. 2B) twice, k. 1B, (k. 10M, k. 1B, p. 2B, k. 2B, p. 2B, k. 1B) to end, but ending last repeat p. 2B, k. 2B.
16th row: (P. 2B, k. 2B) twice, p. 1B, (p. 10M, p. 1B, k. 2B, p. 2B, k. 2B, p. 1B) to end, but ending last repeat k. 2B, p. 2B.
17th row: As 15th.
18th and 19th rows: As 12th and 13th.
20th row: As 12th.
21st and 30th rows: As 1st to 10th but using C in place of A.
31st to 40th rows: As 11th to 20th but using A in place of B and B in place of M.
These 40 rows form patt.
Continue in patt. until work measures 55 (66; 77) cm., 21¾ (26; 30½) in., ending after a wrong-side row.

Keeping patt. correct, shape neck thus:–
Next row: Patt. 47 (54; 61), cast off centre 24 (28;32) sts., patt. to end.
Continue on last group. Dec. 1 st. at neck edge on next 5 rows. 42 (49; 56) sts.
Work straight until front measures 61 (74; 56) cm., 24 (29; 34) in. from beg., ending at side edge.
Shape shoulder by casting off 10 (12; 14) sts. at beg. of next and 2 following alt. rows.
Work 1 row. Cast off.
With wrong side facing, rejoin yarn to remaining sts. and complete as first half.

Back
Omitting neck shaping, work as front to shoulder shaping, ending after a wrong-side row.
Shape shoulders by casting off 10 (12; 14) sts. at beg. of next 6 rows, then 12 (13; 14) sts. at beg. of next 2 rows. Cast off.

Sleeves
With No. 10 (3¼ mm) needles and M, cast on 36 (40; 44) sts. Work in rib as on welt for 5 (6; 6) cm., 2 (2½; 2½) in., ending after a 1st row.
Next row: Rib 4 (8; 3), *inc. in next st., rib 2 (0; 1); rep. from * to last 5 (9; 3) sts., inc. in next st., rib to end. 46 (64; 64) sts.
Change to No. 8 (4 mm) needles and patt. as on front, shaping sleeve by inc. 1 st. at each end of 3rd row, then on every following alt. row until there are 82 (86; 96) sts., then on every following 4th row until there are 98 (114; 124) sts., working extra sts. into patt.
Work straight until sleeve measures 36 (41; 44) cm., 14 (16; 17½) in. at centre.
Cast off in 1 colour.

Polo hood
With No. 10 (3¼ mm) needles and M, cast on 180 (188; 196) sts. Work in rib as on welt for 43 (47; 51) cm., 17 (18½; 20) in. Cast off evenly in rib.

TO MAKE UP
Do not press. Join shoulders. Stitch cast-off edges of sleeves to yoke. Join side and sleeve seams. Join side edges of hood, then stitch in position to neck edge.

LEG WARMERS
With No. 10 (3¼ mm) needles and M, cast on 76 (84; 88) sts.
Working in stripes of k. 2, p. 2 rib as on front of Dress work 8 rows M, 8 rows A, 8 rows B, 8 rows C repeated throughout work for 6 cm. (2½ in.) ending after a 2nd row.
Change to No. 8 (4 mm) needles and beg. 2nd row again continue in rib shaping leg by dec. 1 st. at each end of 5th row, then on every following 6th row until 60 (64; 68) sts. remain.
Work straight until work measures 27 (29; 32) cm., 10½ (11½; 12½) in. from beg., ending after a 2nd row.
Change to No. 10 (3¼ mm) needles and beg. 2nd row again work in rib for a further 6 cm. (2½ in.). Cast off in colour of last row.
Join seam.

Angela Douglas

MOTHER OF PEARL DRESS AND COAT

Lovely actress and best-selling author Angela Douglas (widow of the late lamented Kenneth More) chooses her easygoing elegant clothes to match a demanding lifestyle – and to flatter her exceedingly good legs. This stunning dress and coat combination is perfect for formal and casual occasions.

MATERIALS					
Patons Cotton Perle					
Dress	**50 g. balls**	17	17	18	18
Coat	**50 g. balls**	17	17	18	18

Pair long Milward needles each Nos. 9 (3¾ mm) and 11 (3 mm). Set of four No. 11 (3 mm) needles. 7 buttons.

MEASUREMENTS					
To fit bust	**cm.**	81	86	91	97
	in.	32	34	36	38
Dress					
Length from top of shoulder, adjustable	**cm.**	97	97	98	98
	in.	38	38	38½	38½
Sleeve seam, excluding underarm shaping	**cm.**	37	37	37	37
	in.	14½	14½	14½	14½
Coat					
Length from shoulder, adjustable	**cm.**	100	100	100	100
	in.	39½	39½	39½	39½
Sleeve seam	**cm.**	42	42	42	42
	in.	16½	16½	16½	16½

TENSION

23 sts. and 30 rows to 10 cm. (4 in.) over stocking stitch on No. 9 (3¾ mm) needles.

ABBREVIATIONS

k., knit; **p.**, purl; **sts.**, stitches; **st.st.**, stocking st.; **m.1**, make 1 by picking up and knitting into back of horizontal strand lying before next st.; **inc.**, increase, increasing; **dec.**, decrease, decreasing; **beg.**, beginning; **alt.**, alternate; **rep.**, repeat; **cm.**, centimetres; **in.**, inches.

DRESS

Front and Back (2 pieces alike)

With No. 11 (3 mm) needles, cast on 108 (114; 120; 126) sts.

Knit 2 rows.

Next row: K. 4 (7; 10; 13), (m.1, k. 11) 9 times, m.1, k. to end. 118 (124; 130; 136) sts.

Change to No. 9 (3¾ mm) needles and st.st., beg. k. row, until work measures 63 cm. (25 in.), ending after a p. row. (**N.B.** length may be adjusted here.)

Shape underarm and sleeve by inc. 1 st. at each end of next 15 rows. Now cast on 67 sts. loosely at each end of next row. 282 (288; 294; 300) sts.

Continue straight until work measures 11 (12; 13; 13) cm., 4½ (4¾; 5; 5¼) in. from 67 cast-on sts., ending after a p. row.

Shape sleeve top and shoulder by casting off 4 sts. at beg. of every row until 154 (160; 166; 172) sts. remain.

Shape neck, still shaping shoulders, thus:

Next row: Cast off 4 sts., k. 53 (56; 59; 62) – including st. on needle after cast-off, turn.

Continue on this group.

Dec. 1 st. at neck edge on next 4 rows, at the same time casting off 4 sts. at beg. of 2nd and 4th of these rows. 41 (44; 47; 50) sts.

Keeping neck edge straight, continue casting off 4 sts. at beg. of every alt. row until 17 (20; 23; 26) sts. remain. Work 1 row. Cast off.

With wrong side facing, slip centre 40 sts. on a spare needle. Rejoin yarn to remaining sts. and k. to end.

Work 4 rows, casting off 4 sts. at beg. of 1st and 3rd rows and dec. 1 st. at neck edge on every row. 41 (44; 47; 50) sts.

Complete as first half.

Neck Edging

First join shoulders. With set of No. 11 (3 mm) needles, right side facing, k. up 144 sts. evenly round neck, including sts. on spare needles. Purl 1 round. Knit 1 round. Now turn work inside out and cast off evenly knitways.

Cuffs
With No. 11 (3 mm) needles, right side facing, k. up 43 (45; 49; 51) sts. evenly and firmly along lower edge of sleeve.
1st row: K. 1, (p. 1, k. 1) to end.
2nd row: K. 2, (p. 1, k. 1) to last st., k. 1.
Rep. these 2 rows for 7 cm. (3 in.). Cast off evenly in rib.

TO MAKE UP
Do not press. Join side and sleeve seams.

COAT
Right Front
With No. 11 (3 mm) needles, cast on 59 (61; 65; 67) sts.
1st row: K. 2, (p. 1, k. 1) to last st., k. 1.
2nd row: K. 1, (p. 1, k. 1) to end.
Rep. these 2 rows for 4 cm. (1½ in.), ending after a 2nd row and inc. 1 st. at side edge on 2nd and 4th sizes only on last row. 59 (62; 65; 68) sts.
Change to No. 9 (3¾ mm) needles and st.st., beg. k. row, until work measures 63 cm. (25 in.) from beg., ending after a p. row.
Shape front slope thus:
Dec. 1 st. at front edge on next and every following 6th row until 53 (56; 59; 62) sts. remain.
Shape armhole thus:
Next row: Cast off 6 (7; 8; 9) sts., p. to end.
**Still dec. at front edge on every 6th row from previous dec., at the same time dec. 1 st. at armhole edge on every k. row until 39 (41; 43; 45) sts. remain.
Now dec. 1 st. at *both* edges on every following 6th row until 27 (27; 29; 31) sts. remain.
1st size only:
Work 6 rows dec. 1 st. at armhole edge only on 6th row.
3rd size only:
Work 6 rows dec. 1 st. at front edge only on 6th row.
4th size only:
Work 12 rows dec. 1 st. at front edge only on 6th and 12th rows.
All sizes:
26 (27; 28; 29) sts. Work straight until front

measures 23 (24; 25; 27) cm., 9 (9½; 10; 10½) in. from beg. of armhole shaping, ending at armhole edge.
Shape shoulder by casting off 9 (9; 9; 10) sts. at beg. of next and following alt. row.
Work 1 row. Cast off.

Left Front
Work as right front up to front slope shaping.
Shape front slope thus:
Dec. 1 st. at front edge on next and every following 6th row until 54 (57; 60; 63) sts. remain.
Work 5 rows straight.
Shape armhole thus:
Next row: Cast off 6 (7; 8; 9) sts., k. to last 2 sts., k. 2 together.
Next row: P.
Complete as right front working from ** to end.

Back
With No. 11 (3 mm) needles, cast on 121 (127; 133; 139) sts.
Work in rib as on right front for 4 cm. (1½ in.), ending after a 2nd row but inc. 1 st. at end of last row on all sizes. 122 (128; 134; 140) sts.
Change to No. 9 (3¾ mm) needles and beg. k. row work in st.st. until back measures same as left front up to armhole shaping, thus ending after a p. row.
Shape armholes by casting off 6 (7; 8; 9) sts. at beg. of next 2 rows. Dec. 1 st. at each end of every k. row until 98 (102; 106; 110) sts. remain, then at each end of every following 6th row until 84 (88; 92; 96) sts. remain.
Work straight until back measures 27 (28; 29; 30) cm., 10½ (11; 11½; 12) in. from beg. of armhole shaping, ending after a p. row. (**N.B.** Back armhole is longer than front to allow for saddle).
Shape shoulders by casting off 9 (9; 9; 10) sts. at beg. of next 4 rows, then 8 (9; 10; 9) sts. at beg. of next 2 rows. Slip final 32 (34; 36; 38) sts. on a length of yarn.

Right Sleeve
With No. 11 (3 mm) needles, cast on 43 (45; 47; 49) sts. Work in rib as on right front for 4 cm. (1½ in.), ending after a 2nd row and inc. 1 (5; 7; 11) sts. evenly on last row. 44 (50; 54; 60) sts.
Change to No. 9 (3¾ mm) needles and beg. k. row work in st.st., shaping sleeve by inc. 1 st. at each end of 3rd row, then on every following 4th row until there are 68 (74; 78; 84) sts., then on every following 6th row until there are 82 (88; 92; 98) sts.
Work straight until sleeve measures 37 cm. (14½ in.) at centre, ending after a p. row.
Now inc. 1 st. at each end of every k. row until there are 96 (102; 106; 112) sts.
Purl 1 row.
Shape top by casting off 6 (7; 8; 9) sts. at beg. of next 2 rows. Dec. 1 st. at each end of next (next; 3rd; 3rd) row, then on every following k. row until 66 sts. remain.
Purl 1 row.
Now cast off 3 sts. at beg. of every row until 36 sts. remain.
Next row: Cast off 8 sts., k. to end.
Next row: Cast off 18 sts., p. to end.
Continue on remaining 10 sts. for 34 (35; 36; 37) rows. Slip sts. on a spare needle.

Left Sleeve
Work as right sleeve until 36 sts. remain.
Next row: Cast off 18 sts., k. to end.
Next row: Cast off 8 sts., p. to end.
Complete as right sleeve.

Pockets (2)
With No. 9 (3¾ mm) needles, cast on 51 sts.
Beg. k. row, work in st.st. for 18 cm. (7¼ in.), ending after a p. row and noting that p. rows should begin and end 'k. 1'.
Change to No. 11 (3 mm) needles and work 10 rows as on right front. Cast off loosely in rib.

Right Half of Border
First join saddles to front and back shoulders, then stitch top of sleeves to armholes. With No. 11 (3 mm) needles, right side facing, k. up 10 sts. from edge of right welt, 140 sts. evenly spaced up to start of front slope, 77 (80; 83; 86) sts. up to saddle, k. across 10 sts. of saddle, finally k. across first 16 (17; 18; 19) sts. on length of yarn at back of neck. 253 (257; 261; 265) sts. (**N.B.** A 3rd No. 11 (3 mm) needle may be used to hold sts. if required).
Beg. 2nd row work 3 rows in rib as on welt.
Next row: (buttonhole row): Rib 4, (cast off 3 sts. neatly in rib, rib 21 – including st. on needle after cast-off) 6 times, cast off 3 sts., rib to end.
Next row: In rib, casting on 3 sts. in each place where sts., were cast off.
Work 3 more rows in rib. Cast off evenly in rib.

Left Half of Border
Commencing at back of neck and omitting holes, work to correspond with right half.

TO MAKE UP
Do not press. Join side and sleeve seams. Join ends of borders at back of neck. Sew on pockets and buttons.

Bonnie Langford

BUNCH OF GRAPES SWEATER

She can dance like a star, sing like a star and this tiny girl who has made her West End mark in countless productions, including *Pirates of Penzance*, is just twenty-one. Off stage she chooses racy, mad teenage clothes.

MATERIALS

Patons Mohair Focus (**MS**)	**25 g. balls**	13
Patons Mohair Focus (**C**)	**25 g. balls**	5

Pair long Milward needles each Nos. 4 (6 mm) and 8 (4 mm).

MEASUREMENTS

To fit bust	**cm.**	81–86
	in.	32–34
Length at centre front, excluding collar	**cm.**	49
	in.	19½

TENSION
14 sts. and 19 rows to 10 cm. (4 in.) over reversed stocking stitch using MS and No. 4 (6 mm) needles.

ABBREVIATIONS
k., knit; **p.**, purl; **sts.**, stitches; **rev.st.st.**, reversed stocking st.; **patt.**, pattern; **dec.**, decrease, decreasing; **beg.**, beginning; **tog.**, together; **rep.**, repeat; **m.b.**, make bobble in C thus: cast on 6 sts. to left needle as follows: *insert right needle into st. on left needle and knit a new st., now put this st. back on left needle; rep. from * until 6 new sts. in all have been cast on, now still in C, k. the 6 new sts. and then drop the original st. (7th stitch), finally slip the 2nd, 3rd, 4th, 5th and 6th stitches one by one over the first st.; **cm.**, centimetres; **in.**, inches; **MS**, Main Shade; **C**, Contrast.

PANEL (worked over 7 sts.)
(**N.B.:** When going from a p. stitch in MS to a k. stitch or a bobble stitch in C keep MS at wrong side of work.)
1st row (right side): P. 3 MS, k. 1 C, p. 3 MS.
2nd row: K. 3 MS, p. 1 C, k. 3 MS.
3rd to 8th rows: Rep. 1st and 2nd rows 3 times.
9th row: P. 3 MS, m.b. C, p. 3 MS.
10th row: K. 3 MS, p. 1 MS, k. 3 MS.
11th row: P. 2 MS, m.b. C, p. 1 MS, m.b. C, p. 2 MS.
12th row: K. 2 MS, p. 3 MS, k. 2 MS.
13th row: P. 1 MS, (m.b. C, p. 1 MS) 3 times.
14th row: K. 1 MS, p. 5 MS, k. 1 MS.
15th row: m.b. C, (p. 1 MS, m.b. C) 3 times.
16th row: P. 7 MS.
17th and 18th rows: As 13 and 14th.
These 18 rows form panel.

FRONT
With No. 8 (4 mm) needles and MS, cast on 49 sts.
1st row: K. 2, (p. 1, k. 1) to last st., k. 1.
2nd row: K. 1, (p. 1, k. 1) to end.
Rep. these 2 rows for 11 cm. (4½ in.), ending after a 2nd row and casting on 57 sts. at each end of needle on last row. 163 sts.
Change to No. 4 (6 mm) needles and patt. thus:
(**N.B.:** Use a separate ball of C for each panel.)
1st row: P. 6 MS, (work 1st row of panel, p. 11 MS) 8 times, work 1st row of panel, p. 6 MS.
2nd row: K. 6 MS, (work 2nd row of panel, k. 11 MS) 8 times, work 2nd row of panel, k. 6 MS.
3rd to 18th rows: Rep. 1st and 2nd rows 8 times, but working 3rd to 18th rows of panel.
These 18 rows form patt.
Keeping panels and colours correct, shape thus:
1st dec. row: P. 1, p. 2 tog., p. 3, (work 1st row of panel, p. 4, p. 3 tog., p. 4) 8 times, work 1st row of panel, p. 3, p. 2 tog., p. 1. 145 sts.
Work 13 rows straight.
2nd dec. row: P. 1, p. 2 tog., p. 2, (work panel, p. 3, p. 3 tog., p. 3) 8 times, work panel, p. 2, p. 2 tog., p. 1. 127 sts.
Work 11 rows straight.
3rd dec. row: P. 1, p. 2 tog., p. 1, (work panel, p. 2, p. 3 tog., p. 2) 8 times, work panel, p. 1, p. 2 tog., p. 1. 109 sts.
Work 9 rows straight.
4th dec. row: P. 1, p. 2 tog., (work panel, p. 1, p. 3 tog., p. 1) 8 times, work panel, p. 2 tog., p. 1. 91 sts.
Work 7 rows straight.
(**N.B.:** On last row, 8th row of panel has been worked.) Now break C and continue in MS only thus:
5th dec. row: P. 2 tog., (p. 3, k. 1, p. 3, p. 3 tog.) 8 times, p. 3, k. 1, p. 3, p. 2 tog. 73 sts.
Beg. with a k. row continue in rev.st.st. on all sts. until work measures 38 cm. (15 in.) from top of rib, ending after a k. row.
Next row: P. 1, (p. 2 tog., p. 1) to end. 49 sts.
Next row: K. 1, (k. 2 tog., k. 3) 9 times, k. 2 tog., k. 1. 39 sts.
Change to No. 8 (4 mm) needles and beg. with *1st row* work in rib as on welt for 19 cm. (7½ in.). Cast off loosely in rib.

BACK
Work as front.

CUFFS
First join shoulders and neckband. Place a marker 15 cm. (6 in.) at both sides of lower edge of shoulder seam. With No. 8 (4 mm) needles and MS, right side facing, k. up 35 sts. evenly spaced between one set of markers. Beg. with 2nd row work in rib for 7 cm. (3 in.). Cast off loosely in rib.
Work other cuff to match.

TO MAKE UP
Do not press. Join cuffs and cast-on edges of back and front as far as top of welt, finally join welt.

John Inman

YELLOW AND GREEN COTTON SWEATER

As everybody's favourite comedy salesman, Mr Humphries of *Are You Being Served,* John Inman turns gents clothing into pure horror. In real life Mr Inman is an elegant connoisseur of unusual colours. Here he chooses a pale yellow cotton sweater with a dash of green 'for casual summer evenings'.

MATERIALS				
Patons Cotton Top **(MS)** 6420	**50 g. balls**	7	8	9
(C) 6443	**50 g. balls**	2	2	2
Pair each No. 10 (3¼ mm) No. 7 (4½ mm) and No. 6 (5 mm) knitting needles.				
MEASUREMENTS				
To fit chest	**cm.**	91	97	102
	in.	36	38	40
Length from top of shoulders	**cm.**	61	62	63
	in.	24	24½	25
Sleeve seam	**cm.**	48	48	49
	in.	19	19	19

TENSION
18 sts. and 26 rows to 10 cm. (4 in.) measured over rev.st.st. on No. 6 (5 mm) needles.

ABBREVIATIONS
k., knit; **p.**, purl; **st.**, stitch; **rev.st.st.**, reverse stocking stitch; **inc.**, increase; **beg.**, beginning; **cont.**, continue; **foll.**, following; **r.s.**, right side; **w.s.**, wrong side; **cm.**, centimetres; **mm.**, millimetres; **in.**, inches; **ms.**, main shade; **C.**, contrast; **m.1**, make 1 stitch by picking up horizontal loop lying before next stitch and working into back of it.

BACK AND FRONT (THE SAME)
With No. 10 (3¼ mm) needles and MS. cast on 80 (86; 90) sts. and work in k. 1, p. 1 rib for 7 cm. (2¾ in.).
Next row: Rib 5 (3; 5), m.1, [rib 7 (8; 8), m.1] 10 times, rib 5 (3; 5). [91 (97; 101) sts.]
Change to No. 6 (5 mm) needles and starting with a p. row, work in rev.st.st. until back measures 56.5 (57.5; 58.5) cm. 22 (22½; 23) in., ending with r.s. facing. Break MS.
Change to No. 7 (4½ mm) needles and using C., k. 1 row.
Cont. in p. 1, k. 1 rib, rows on w.s. having a p. 1 at each end, for 4.5 cm. (2 in.), ending with r.s. facing.
Cast off neatly in rib.

SLEEVES
With No. 10 (3¼ mm) needles and MS., cast on 42 (44; 46) sts. and work in k. 1, p. 1 rib for 6 cm. (2½ in.).
Next row: Rib 3 (4; 5), m. 1, [rib 4, m.1] 9 times, rib 3 (4; 5). [52 (54; 56) sts.]
Change to No. 6 (5 mm) needles and using separate balls of yarn as required, twisting yarns on w.s. to avoid a hole, work as folls.:
1st row: P. 18 (19; 20) MS., k. 16 C., p. 18 (19; 20) MS.
2nd row: K. 18 (19; 20) MS., k. 16 C., k. 18 (19; 20) MS
3rd row: P. 18 (19; 20) MS., p. 16 C., p. 18 (19; 20) MS.
2nd and 3rd rows form patt.
Shape sides by inc. 1 st. at each end of next and every foll. 5th row until there are 86 (90; 94) sts. taking inc. sts. into MS.
Work straight until sleeve measures 48 (48; 49) cm. 19 (19; 19) in. ending with r.s. facing.
Cast off.

MAKE UP
Do not press.
Join shoulders, leaving a gap of 33 cm. (13 in.) at centre for head opening.
Matching band of C. on sleeves with neckline ribbing, sew in sleeves down side edges of front and back.
Join side and sleeve seams.

Molly Parkin

TUDOR JACKET AND 1985 HAT

Molly Parkin, comedienne, poet, novelist and chat show stirrer, always dresses to cause a sensation. This red and black striped woollen jacket with its dramatic sleeves is no exception, and the hat adds a final note of triumph to an outfit designed for any dresser with flair.

MATERIALS

Patons Beehive Chunky

Coat,	Dark **(D)**	**50 g. balls**	15	16	17
	Light **(L)**	**50 g. balls**	6	6	6
Hat,	Dark **(D)**	**50 g. balls**	1	1	1
	Light **(L)**	**50 g. balls**	1	1	1

Pair Milward needles each Nos. 4 (6 mm) and 6 (5 mm). 3 buttons for coat; length of elastic approximately 41 cm. (16 in.) long and kapok or similar material for stuffing hat rouleau.

MEASUREMENTS

To fit bust	**cm.**	86	91	97
	in.	34	36	38
Length from shoulder	**cm.**	88	89	90
	in.	34½	35	35½
Sleeve seam, approximately	**cm.**	47	47	47
	in.	18½	18½	18½

TENSION

15 sts. and 20 rows to 10 cm. (4 in.) over stocking stitch on No. 4 (6 mm) needles.

ABBREVIATIONS

k., knit; **p.**, purl; **sts.**, stitches; **st.st.**, stocking st.; **m.1**, make 1 by picking up and knitting into back of horizontal thread lying before next st.; **inc.**, increase, increasing; **dec.**, decrease, decreasing; **tog.**, together; **t.b.l.**, through back of loops; **beg.**, beginning; **alt.**, alternate; **rep.**, repeat; **cm.**, centimetres; **in.**, inches.

COAT

Back

With No. 6 (5 mm) needles and D, cast on 84 (88; 92) sts. Work 6 rows in garter st.

Next row: K. 2 (4; 6), (m.1, k. 8) 10 times, m.1, k. to end. 95 (99; 103) sts.

Change to No. 4 (6 mm) needles and beg. k. row work 16 rows in st.st.

Shape thus:–

Dec. row: K. 15, k. 2 tog. t.b.l., k. 3, k. 2 tog., k. to last 22 sts., k. 2 tog. t.b.l., k. 3, k.2 tog., k. 15. (4 sts. decreased).

Work 15 rows straight.

Rep. the last 16 rows until 75 (79; 83) sts. remain.

Work straight until back measures 66 cm. (26 in.) from beg., ending after a p. row.

Shape armholes by casting off 6 (7; 8) sts. at beg. of next 2 rows.

Dec. 1 st. at each end of next 3 k. rows. 57 (59; 61) sts.

Work straight until back measures 88 (89; 90) cm., 34½ (35; 35½) in. at centre, from beg., ending after a p. row.

Shape shoulders by casting off 5 sts. at beg. of next 4 rows, then 5 (6; 6) sts. at beg. of next 2 rows. Cast off final 27 (27; 29) sts.

Right front

With No. 6 (5 mm) needles and D, cast on 42 (44; 46) sts. Work 6 rows in garter st.

Next row: K. 5 (6; 7), (m.1, k. 8) 4 times, m.1, k. to end. 47 (49; 51) sts.

Change to No. 4 (6 mm) needles and beg. k. row work 16 rows in st.st.

Shape thus:–

Dec. row: K. to last 22 sts., k. 2 tog. t.b.l., k. 3, k. 2 tog., k. 15. (2 sts. decreased).

Work 15 rows straight.

Rep. the last 16 rows until 37 (39; 41) sts. remain.

Work straight until front measures 38 rows less than back up to armhole shaping.

Shape front slope by dec. 1 st. at front edge on next row, then every following 6th row until 30 (32; 34) sts. remain.

Work 2 rows straight. (N.B.: Work 1 row only on left front).

Shape armhole thus:–

Next row: Cast off 6 (7; 8) sts., p. to end.

**Dec. 1 st. at armhole edge on next 3 k. rows, at the same time dec. 1 st. at front edge on 3rd row following. 20 (21; 22) sts.

Continue dec. at front edge only but on 4th row following then on every following 6th row until 15 (16; 16) sts. remain.

Work straight until front measures 21 (23; 24) cm., 8½ (9; 9½) in. from beg. of armhole shaping, ending at armhole edge.

Shape shoulder by casting off 5 sts. at beg. of next and following alt. row. Work 1 row.

Cast off.

Left front

Work as right front up to armhole shaping but noting that dec. row will be: k. 15, k. 2 tog. t.b.l., k. 3, k. 2 tog., k. to end.

Shape armholes thus:–

Next row: Cast off 6 (7; 8) sts., k. to end.

Purl 1 row. Complete as right front working from ** to end.

Sleeves

Commence with upper section, worked sideways.

With No. 4 (6 mm) needles and L, cast on 47 sts. Joining in and breaking off colours as required, work in ridged stripes with shaping thus:–

1st row: In L, k.

2nd row: In L, k.

3rd row: In L, inc. in first st., p. to end.

4th row: In L, k.

5th row: In L, p.

6th to 11th rows: Rep. 2nd to 5th rows once, then 2nd and 3rd rows again.

12th row: In D, p.

13th row: In D, k.

14th row: In D, p.

15th row: In D, inc. in first st. k. to end.

16th to 20th rows: Rep. 12th to 15th rows once, then 12th row again. (52 sts.)

Rep. 1st to 20th rows once more.

Continue in stripes but inc. 1 st. at shaped edge on 5th row following, then on every following 6th row until there are 60 sts.

Work 37 rows straight, thus ending after 3 rows D.

Continue in ridged stripes shaping 2nd half of sleeve by dec. 1 st. at beg. of next row, then on every following 6th row until 56 sts. remain, then on every following 4th row until 47 sts. remain. Work 1 row. Cast off.

With right side facing and No. 6 (5 mm) needles

and D., k. up 45 (47; 49) sts. evenly along lower edge of sleeve (i.e. edge opposite the shaped edge).
1st row: K. 1, (p. 1, k. 1) to end.
2nd row: K. 2, (p. 1, k. 1) to last st., k. 1.
Continue in rib dec. 1 st. at each end of next row, then on every following 4th row until 37 (39; 41) sts. remain, then on every following 6th row until 33 (35; 37) sts. remain.
Work straight until rib measures 18 cm. (7 in.) or desired length. Cast off loosely in rib.

Right half of collar
With No. 4 (6 mm) needles and D, cast on 3 sts.
1st row: In D, inc. in first st., k. to end.
2nd row: In D, p.
3rd to 8th rows: Rep. 1st and 2nd rows 3 times.
9th row: In L, as 1st.
10th row: In L, k. to end.
11th row: In L, inc. in first st., p. to end.
12th to 19th rows: Rep. 10th and 11th rows 4 times.
20th row: In D, p.
Rep. these 20 rows until there are 22 sts.
Continue straight for 60 (64; 68) rows. Cast off with colour of last row.

Left half of collar
Work as right half but working shapings at opposite edge.

Border
With No. 6 (5 mm) needles and D, right side facing, k. up 87 (91; 95) sts. *evenly spaced* along outer (i.e. straight) edge of one collar piece.
Work 6 rows in rib as on sleeves. Cast off loosely and evenly in rib.
Work 2nd half the same.

To make up
Do not press. Join shoulder, side and sleeve seams. Sew in sleeves gathering up sleeve top to fit armhole. Sew on collar joining ends at back of next and joining side edges of rib to side edges of ribbed front borders. Sew on buttons.

HAT
To make
With No. 4 (6 mm) needles and L, cast on 12 sts.
K. 1 row. Now beg. k. row again work 10 rows in reversed st.st. Break L. Join in D. Beg. p. row work 10 rows in st.st.
Rep. these 20 rows for approximately 122 cm. (48 in.), ending after a stripe in D or L.
Cast off in appropriate colour.
Join side edges to form a tube, inserting kapok to form a rouleau as you go. Wind and twist together to form a "snake" effect as in photograph, securing where necessary.
Attach to length of elastic.

GFH

Gary Holton

STREET-WISE MOHAIR BEATNIK SWEATER

Gary Holton likes tight jeans, big beatnik tops and vicious dark glasses. Holton, comedy actor and star of television's *Auf Wiedersehen Pet*, designed this beatnik sweater for those with a similar taste for the street-wise look. Combining comfort and style, it is equally attractive on men and women.

MATERIALS						
Patons Mohair Focus (**MS**) 2082	**25 g. balls**	9	10	10	11	11
(**C**) 2090	**25 g. balls**	7	8	8	9	9
Pair each No. 7 (4½ mm) and No. 5 (5½ mm) knitting needles						
MEASUREMENTS						
To fit bust/chest	**cm.**	81	86	91	97	102
	in.	32	34	36	38	40
Length from top of shoulders	**cm.**	78	78	80	80	80
	in.	31	31	31½	31½	31½
Sleeve seam	**cm.**	54	54	54	54	54
	in.	21	21	21	21	21

TENSION
15 sts. and 20 rows to 10 cm. (4 in.) measured over st.st. on No. 5 (5½ mm) needles.

ABBREVIATIONS
k., knit; **p.**, purl; **st.** stitch; **st.st.**, stocking stitch; **tog.**, together; **inc.**, increase; **dec.**, decrease; **beg.**, beginning; **alt.**, alternate; **rep.**, repeat; **patt.**, pattern; **cont.**, continue; **foll.**, following; **rem.**, remaining; **r.s.**, right side; **w.s.**, wrong side; **cm.**, centimetres; **mm.**, millimetres; **in.**, inches; **MS.**, Main Shade; **C.**, Contrast; **m.1.**, make 1 stitch by picking up horizontal loop lying before next stitch and working into back of it.

STRIPE PATT.
24 rows C., 24 rows MS.
These 48 rows form stripe patt.

BACK
**With No. 7 (4½ mm) needles and MS, cast on 58 (62; 66; 70; 74) sts. and work in rib as folls:
1st row: (R.S.), k. 2, *p. 2, k. 2; rep. from * to end.
2nd row: P. 2, *k. 2, p. 2; rep. from * to end.
These 2 rows form ribbing, work until ribbing measures 8 cm, (3 in.) ending with 1st row.
Next row: Rib 2 (4; 1; 3; 1), m. 1, [rib 6 (6; 7; 7; 8), m.1] 9 times, rib 2 (4; 2; 4; 1). [68 (72; 76; 80; 84) sts.]**
Change to No. 5 (5½ mm) needles and work in st.st. and stripe patt., joining in and breaking off colours as required, until back measures 78 (78; 80; 80; 80) cm. 31 (31; 31½; 31½; 31½) in., ending with r.s. facing.
Cast off 15 (16; 17; 18; 19) sts. at beg of next 2 rows.
Leave rem. 38 (40; 42; 44; 46) sts. on a spare needle.

FRONT
Work as for back from ** to **.
Change to No. 5 (5½ mm) needles and work in st.st. and stripe patt., until front matches back to shoulder less 16 (16, 18, 18; 18) rows, thus ending with r.s. facing.
Divide for neck, keeping stripe patt. correct, as folls.:
Next row: K. 22 (24; 25; 27; 28), k. 2 tog. turn and leave rem. sts. on a spare needle.
Dec. 1 st. at neck edge until 15 (16; 17; 18; 19) sts. rem.
Work straight until front matches back to shoulder, ending with r.s. facing.
Cast off rem. sts.
With r.s. facing, slip centre 20 (20; 22; 22; 24) sts. on a spare needle, rejoin appropriate colour to rem. sts., k. 2 tog., k. to end.
Work to match first side, reversing shapings.

SLEEVES
With No. 7 (4½ mm) needles and MS., cast on 38 (42; 42; 46; 46) sts. and work in k. 2, p. 2 rib as given for lower edge on back for 12 cm. (5 in.) ending with 1st row.
Next row: Rib 2 (3; 2; 3; 2), m.1, [rib 1, m.1] 33 (35; 37; 39; 41) times, rib 3 (4; 3; 4; 3). [72 (76; 80; 84; 88) sts.]
Change to No. 5 (5½ mm) needles and work in st.st. and stripe patt. until sleeve measures 54 cm. (21 in.), ending with r.s. facing.
Cast off.

MAKE UP AND NECK BORDER
Do not press.
Join right shoulder seam.

NECK BORDER
With r.s. facing, No. 7 (4½ mm) needles and MS, *knit up* 14 (15; 15; 16; 17) sts. down left side of neck, k. 20 (20; 22; 22; 24) sts. from front, *knit up* 14 (15; 15; 16; 17) sts. up right side of neck, k. 38 (40; 42; 44; 46) sts. from back. [86 (90; 94; 98; 102) sts.].
Starting with 2nd row, work in rib as given for lower edge on back, for 5 cm. (2 in.) ending with r.s. facing.
using a No. 5 (5½ mm) needle, cast off loosely in rib.
Join left shoulder and neck border. Fold neck border in half and stitch in position.
Place centre of sleeve to shoulder and sew in down side edges of front and back.
Join side and sleeve seams.
With an oddment of black 4 ply, embroider initials and emblem as in photograph.

Three Degrees

HEAD START IN THE CHARTS

Fame has certainly not gone to the heads of Prince Charles's favourite girl rock group (remember *When Will I See You Again*). Sheila Ferguson, Valerie Holiday and Helen Scott went wild over these designs and let them go to their heads in the most flattering way.

HEADBANDS

MATERIALS

Two-colour Twisted Headband		
Patons Solo DK	**50 g. balls**	1
1 ball each in 2 contrasting colours		
Plaited Headband		
Patons Solo DK	**50 g. balls**	2

Pair No. 8 (4 mm) needles. Kapok or similar material for stuffing.

MEASUREMENTS
To fit an average woman's head

TENSION
22 sts. and 30 rows to 10 cm. (4 in.) over reversed stocking stitch.

ABBREVIATIONS
sts., stitches; **rev.st.st.**, reversed stocking stitch; **cm.**, centimetres; **in.**, inches.

PLAITED HEADBAND
Main Part
Make 3 strips as follows:
Cast on 16 sts. Work in rev.st.st. for approximately 81 cm. (32 in.).
Cast off.
Make 2 more strips the same.

Ring
Cast on 22 sts. Work in rev.st.st. for approximately 14 cm. (5½ in.).
Cast off.

To Complete
Do not press. Join side edges of each of the 3 long strips to form 3 'tubes' inserting kapok as you go to form a 'sausage' effect joining cast-on edges of each. Now catch cast-off end of each 'tube' together and make a plait. Sew into a ring adjusting lengths of 'tubes' if necessary. ** Finally, join side edges of ring then wrap around the join in headband and neatly catch ends together on wrong side. **

TWO-COLOUR TWISTED HEADBAND
To Make
With 1st colour, cast on 18 sts. Work in rev.st.st. for approximately 71 cm. (28 in.). Cast off. Make another piece the same but using 2nd colour. Make ring in either colour as for plaited headband.

To Complete
Do not press. Join side edges of each strip to form 2 'tubes' inserting kapok as you go to form a 'sausage' effect. Now catch one end of each tube together and twist the 2 'tubes' around each other, sewing ends together to form a ring. Work as plaited headband from ** to **.

THREE RIBBED SCARVES

MATERIALS

Patons Solo DK, **One-colour version**		**50 g. balls**	11
Two-colour version	**A**	**50 g. balls**	5
	B	**50 g. balls**	5
Four-colour version	**A**	**50 g. balls**	8
	B	**50 g. balls**	1
	C	**50 g. balls**	1
	D	**50 g. balls**	1

Pair No. 8 (4 mm) Milward needles. Medium crochet hook for one-colour version.

MEASUREMENTS

Width, not stretched, approximately	**cm.**	40
	in.	15¾
Length, approximately (excluding fringe on one-colour version)	**cm.**	220
	in.	87

TENSION
36 sts. in width to 10 cm. (4 in.) over rib not stretched.

ABBREVIATIONS
k., knit; **p.**, purl; **sts.**, stitches; **rep.**, repeat; **cm.**, centimetres; **in.**, inches.

ONE-COLOUR VERSION
Cast on 144 sts.
1st row: K. 3, (p. 2, k. 2) to last st., k. 1.
2nd row: K. 1, (p. 2, k. 2) to last 3 sts., p. 2, k. 1.
Rep. these 2 rows for approximately 220 cm. (87 in.). Cast off in rib.
Cut remainder of yarn into approximately 30 cm. (12 in.) lengths and taking 3 strands for every tassel, using the crochet hook, fringe the 2 short ends.
Do not press. Trim tassels evenly.

TWO-COLOUR VERSION
Omitting fringe, work as one-colour version, casting on in A and working in stripes of 12 rows A, 12 rows B, repeated throughout, ending after 12 rows A. Cast off in rib in A.

FOUR-COLOUR VERSION
Omitting fringe, work as one-colour version, casting on in A and working in stripes repeated throughout of 16 rows A, 4 rows B, 16 rows A, 4 rows C, 16 rows A, 4 rows D, ending after 16 rows A. Cast off in rib in A.

FINGERLESS GLOVES

MATERIALS

Patons Solo DK	**50 g. balls**	1

Pair No. 10 (3¼ mm) Milward Disc needles

MEASUREMENTS

Width above thumb	**cm.**	18
	in.	7
Length approximately	**cm.**	20
	in.	8

TENSION
24 sts. and 32 rows to 10 cm. (4 in.) over stocking stitch.

ABBREVIATIONS
k., knit; **p.**, purl; **sts.**, stitches; **st.st.**,stocking stitch; **g.st.**, garter st.; **inc.**, increase, increasing; **dec.**, decrease, decreasing; **beg.**, beginning; **alt.**, alternate; **rep.**, repeat; **cm.**, centimetres; **in.**, inches.

RIGHT GLOVE
Cast on 39 sts.
1st row: K. 2, (p. 1, k. 1) to last st., k. 1.
2nd row: K. 1, (p. 1, k. 1) to end.
Work 20 more rows in rib inc. 3 sts. evenly across last row. 42 sts. **
Change to st.st. with thumb gusset thus:
1st row: K. 21, p. 1, k. 2, p. 1, k. to end.
2nd and every alt. row: K. 1, p. to last st., k. 1.
3rd row: K. 21, p. 1, inc. twice in next st., k. 1, p. 1, k. to end.
5th row: K. 21, p. 1, k. 4, p. 1. k. to end.
7th row: K. 21, p. 1, (inc. in next st., k. 1) twice, p. 1 k. to end.
9th row: K. 21, p. 1, k. 6, p. 1, k. to end.
11th row: K. 21, p.1, inc. in next st., k. 3, inc. in next st., k. 1, p. 1, k. to end.
Continue inc. 2 sts. in thumb gusset on every following 4th row until 2 more sets of increasings have been worked. 52 sts.
Still working purl st. at each side of thumb gusset, work 5 rows straight.
Divide for thumb thus:
Next row: K. 34, turn.
Next row: K. 1, p. 11, cast on 4 sts. turn.
***Work 6 rows in st.st. on these 16 sts., p. rows having k. 1 at each end.
Work 5 rows in g.st. Cast off. ***
With right side facing, rejoin yarn and k. up 4 sts. from the 4 cast-on sts., k. 18. (44 sts.)
Next row: K. 1, p. 42, k. 1.
Next row: K. 21, k. 2 tog., k. 1, k. 2 tog., k. to end. 42 sts.
Next row: K. 1, p. to last st., k. 1.
Work 8 rows in st.st., p. rows having a 'k. 1' at each end.
Work 1st finger thus:
1st row: K. 27, turn.
2nd row: K. 1, p. 11, cast on 3 sts., turn.
Work from *** to ***.
Work 2nd finger thus:
With right side facing, rejoin yarn and k. up 3 sts. from 3 cast-on sts. at base of 1st finger, k. 5, turn.
Next row: K. 1, p. 12, cast on 2 sts., turn.
Work from *** to ***.
Work 3rd finger thus:
With right side facing, rejoin yarn and k. up 2 sts. from cast-on sts. at base of 2nd finger, k. 5, turn.
Next row: K. 1, p. 11, cast on 3 sts., turn.
Work from *** to ***.
Work 4th finger thus:
With right side facing, rejoin yarn and k. up 3 sts. from cast-on sts. at base of 3rd finger, k. 5, turn.
Next row: K. 1, p. 11, k. 1, turn.
Work from *** to *** on these 13 sts.

LEFT GLOVE
Work as right glove to **.

Change to st.st. with thumb gusset thus:
1st row: K. 17, p. 1, k. 2, p. 1, k. to end.
2nd and every alt. row: K. 1, p. to last st., k. 1.
3rd row: K. 17, p. 1, inc. twice in next st., k. 1, p.1, k. to end.
5th row: K. 17, p. 1, k. 4, p. 1, k. to end.
7th row: K. 17, p. 1, (inc. in next st., k. 1) twice, p. 1, k. to end.
9th row: K. 17, p. 1, k. 6, p. 1, k. to end.
11th row: K. 17, p. 1, inc. in next st., k. 3, inc. in next st., k. 1, p. 1, k. to end.
Continue inc. 2 sts. in thumb gusset on every following 4th row until 2 more sets of increases have been worked. 52 sts.
Still working purl st. at each side of thumb gusset work 5 rows straight.
Divide for thumb thus:
Next row: K. 30, cast on 4 sts., turn.
Next row: K. 1, p. 14, k. 1, turn.
Complete thumb as right glove.
With right side facing, k. up 4 sts. from 4 cast-on sts., k. 22. 44 sts.
Next row: K. 1, p. 42, k. 1.
Next row: K. 17, k. 2 tog., k. 1, k. 2 tog., k. to end. 42 sts.
Next row: K. 1, p. to last st., k. 1.
Work 8 rows in st.st.
Work 1st finger thus:
1st row: K. 27, cast on 3 sts., turn.
2nd row: K. 1, p. 13, k. 1, turn.
Work as right glove from *** to ***.
Work 2nd finger thus:
With right side of work facing, rejoin yarn and k. up 3 sts. from 3 cast-on sts. at base of 1st finger, k. 5, cast on 2 sts., turn.
Next row: K. 1, p. 13, k. 1, turn.
Work as right glove from *** to ***.
Work 3rd finger thus:
With right side of work facing, rejoin yarn and k. up 2 sts. from base of 2nd finger, k. 5 cast on 3 sts., turn.
Next row: K. 1, p. 13, k. 1, turn.
Work as right glove from *** to ***
Work 4th finger thus:
Work as 4th finger of right glove.

TO MAKE UP
Do not press. Using a flat seam join seams.

THREE PULL-UP RIBBED HOODS

MATERIALS

Patons Solo DK, **One-colour version**	**50 g. balls**	6
Two-colour version A	**50 g. balls**	3
B	**50 g. balls**	3
Four-colour version A (MS)	**50 g. balls**	4
B	**50 g. balls**	1
C	**50 g. balls**	1
D	**50 g. balls**	1

Pair No. 8 (4 mm) Milward knitting needles.

MEASUREMENTS

To fit an average womans head	**cm.**	70
Length, not stretched.	**in.**	27½

TENSION
36 sts. in width to 10 cm. (4 in.) over rib *not* stretched.

ABBREVIATIONS
k., knit; **p.**, purl; **sts.**, stitches; **rep.**, repeat; **cm.**, centimetres; **in.**, inches; **MS.**, Main Shade.

ONE-COLOUR VERSION
Cast on 240 sts.
1st row: K. 3, (p. 2, k. 2) to last st., k. 1.
2nd row: K. 1, (p. 2, k. 2) to last 3 sts., p.2, k. 1.
Rep. these 2 rows for 70 cm. (27½ in.). Cast off *loosely* and *evenly.*
Do not press. Join side edges to form a tube.

TWO-COLOUR VERSION
With A, cast on 240 sts. Work as one-colour version but working in stripes of 10 rows A, 10 rows B, repeated throughout and ending after either 10 rows A or 10 rows B.
Cast off in colour of last row.

FOUR-COLOUR VERSION
With A, cast on 240 sts. Work as one-colour version but working in stripes of 10 rows A, 2 rows B, 10 rows A, 2 rows C, 10 rows A, 2 rows D, repeated throughout and ending after 10 rows A. Cast off in A.

Roy Marsden

THE BIG MAN'S CHUNKY JACKET

Roy Marsden is the detective every woman longs to be interrogated by. The six-foot star of award-winning writer P.D. James's extraordinary crime series draws compliments from countless female fans. His one problem? He can't find sweaters big enough to fit in ordinary shops.

MATERIALS

Patons Beehive Chunky with Mountain Wool	**50 g. balls**	20	20	21	21

Pair Milward needles each Nos. 4 (6 mm) and 6 (5 mm). A cable needle. A 70/71 cm. (28 in.) open-ended zip fastener.

MEASUREMENTS

To fit chest	**cm.**	97	102	107	112
	in.	38	40	42	44
Approximate width at underarms	**cm.**	117	122	127	132
	in.	46	48	50	52
Length from shoulder	**cm.**	74	74	75	75
	in.	29	29	29½	29½
Sleeve seam	**cm.**	51	51	51	51
	in.	20	20	20	20

TENSION

Instructions are based on a standard stocking stitch tension of 15 sts. and 20 rows to 10 cm. (4 in.) on No. 4 (6 mm) needles.

ABBREVIATIONS

k., knit; **p.**, purl; **sts.**, stitches; **patt.**, pattern; **inc.**, increase, increasing; **dec.**, decrease, decreasing; **beg.**, beginning; **alt.**, alternate; **rep.**, repeat; **C.B.**, slip next 2 sts. on cable needle to back of work, k. 2, then k. 2 from cable needle; **C.F.**, slip next 2 sts. on cable needle to front of work, k. 2, then k. 2 from cable needle; **tw.2**, k. next 2 sts. together but do not slip off left needle, now k. the first st. again slipping both sts. off needle; **cm.**, centimetres; **in.**, inches.

BACK

With No. 6 (5 mm) needles, cast on 71 (75; 79; 83) sts.

1st row: K. 2, (p. 1, k.1) to last st., k. 1.

2nd row: K. 1, (p. 1, k. 1) to end.

Rep. these 2 rows for 10 cm. (4 in.), ending after a 1st row.

Next row: Rib 5 (7; 9; 11), (inc. in next st., rib 2) 20 times, inc. in next st., rib to end. 92 (96; 100; 104) sts.

Change to No. 4 (6 mm) needles and patt. thus:

1st row (right side): P. 13 (15; 2; 4), *(tw.2, p. 13) 2 (2; 3; 3) times, tw.2*, p. 2, work from * to *, p. 13 (15; 2; 4).

2nd row: K. 13 (15; 2; 4), * (p.2, k. 13) 2 (2; 3; 3) times, p. 2*, k.2, work from * to *, k. 13 (15; 2; 4).

These 2 rows form patt.

Continue in patt. until work measures 74 (74; 75; 75) cm., 29 (29; 29½; 29½) in. at centre, ending after a wrong-side row.

Shape shoulders by casting off 11 (12; 12; 13) sts. at beg. of next 4 rows, then 12 (11; 13; 12) sts. at beg. of next 2 rows. Slip final 24 (26; 26; 28) sts. on a spare needle.

PANEL (worked over 56 sts.)

1st row: K. 4, C.B., C.F., k. 4, p. 1,tw.2, p.1, C.F., k. 8, C.B., p. 1, tw.2, p. 1, k. 4, C.B., C.F., k. 4.

2nd and 4th rows: (P. 16, k. 1, p. 2, k. 1) twice, p. 16.

3rd row: K. 2, C.B., k. 4, C.F., k. 2, p. 1, tw.2, p.1, k. 2, C.F., k. 4, C.B., k. 2, p. 1, tw.2, p. 1, k. 2, C.B., k. 4, C.F., k. 2.

5th row: C.B., k. 8, C.F., p. 1, tw.2, p. 1, k. 4, C.F., C.B., k. 4, p. 1, tw.2, p. 1, C.B., k. 8, C.F.

6th row: As 2nd.

These 6 rows form panel.

RIGHT FRONT

With No. 6 (5 mm) needles, cast on 35 (37; 39; 41) sts. Work in rib as on back for 10 cm. (4 in.), ending after a 1st row.

Next row: Rib – (1; 2; 3), (inc. once in each of next 3 sts., rib 1) 8 times, inc. once in each of next 2 sts., rib to end. 61 (63; 65; 67) sts.

Change to No. 4 (6 mm) needles and patt. thus:

1st and 2nd sizes only:

1st row: P. 1, tw.2, p. 1, work 1st row of panel, p. 1 (3; -; -).

2nd row: K. 1 (3; -; -), work 2nd row of panel, k. 1, p. 3.

3rd to 6th rows: Rep. 1st and 2nd rows twice but working rows 3 to 6 of panel.

3rd and 4th sizes only:

1st row: P. 1, tw.2, p. 1, work 1st row of panel, p. 1, tw.2, p. - (-; 2; 4).

2nd row: K. - (-; 2; 4), p. 2, k. 1, work 2nd row of

panel, k. 1, p. 3.
3rd to 6th rows: Rep. 1st and 2nd rows twice but working rows 3 to 6 of panel.

All sizes:
Continue in patt. as on these 6 rows until work measures 66 cm., (26 in.) at centre, ending at front edge.
Shape neck by casting off 12 (13; 13; 14) sts. at beg. of next row.
Dec. 1 st. at neck edge on next 4 rows. 45 (46; 48; 49) sts.
Work straight until front measures same as back to shoulder shaping, ending at side edge.
Shape shoulder by casting off 15 (15; 16; 16) sts. *firmly* at beg. of next and following alt. row.
Work 1 row. Cast off.

LEFT FRONT
Work to correspond with right front but reversing shaping and patt. rows, thus 1st row for 1st and 2nd sizes will commence: P. 1 (3; -; -), and 1st row for 3rd and 4th sizes will commence: P. - (-; 2; 4).

SLEEVES
With No. 6 (5 mm) needles, cast on 31 (33; 33; 35) sts. Work in rib as on back for 10 cm. (4 in.), ending after a 1st row.
Next row: Rib 5, inc. once in each of next 20 (22; 24; 26) sts., rib to end. 51 (55; 57; 61) sts.
Change to No. 4 (6 mm) needles and patt. thus:
1st row: P. 2 (4; 5; 7), (tw.2, p. 13) 3 times, tw.2, p. 2 (4; 5; 7).
2nd row: K. 2 (4; 5; 7), (p. 2, k. 13) 3 times, p. 2, k. to end.
These 2 rows form patt.
Continue in patt., shaping sleeve by inc. 1 st. at each end of next row, then on every following 6th row until there are 75 (79; 81; 85) sts., taking extra sts. into reversed stocking st. Work straight until sleeve measures 51 cm. (20 in.) at centre. Cast off.

NECKBAND
First join shoulders easing in cables of fronts to fit back shoulders.
With No. 6 (5 mm) needles, k. up 71 (75; 79; 83) sts. evenly round neck including sts. on spare needle.
Beg. 2nd row, work in rib as on back for 11 cm. (4½ in.). Cast off.

TO MAKE UP
Do not press. Stitch cast-off edge of sleeves in position to yoke, then join side and sleeve seams. Sew in zip allowing for neckband to be folded in half. Fold neckband in half to wrong side and hem in position all round.

Polly Hemingway
THE COCKTAIL SUNTOP

Roy Marsden's talented actress wife Polly Hemingway (she played his wife in television's *Airline*) has starred recently in the West End hit play *Why Me?* opposite Richard Briers. Polly likes clothes that do for day but can take her into evening – like this soft little top, perfect for sunny days or cocktail evenings.

MATERIALS

Patons Cotton Soft	**50 g. balls**	8	9	10	11

1 pair needles Nos. 8 (4 mm) and 10 (3¼ mm).
2 buttons × 1.5 cm. (½ in.) diameter.

MEASUREMENTS

To fit bust	**cm.**	81	86	91	96
	in.	32	34	36	38
Length from shoulder to hem	**cm.**	60	62	64	66
	in.	24	24½	25	26
Sleeve seam	**cm.**	44	45	46	47
	in.	17	17½	18	18½

TENSION
22 sts. and 29 rows to 10 cm. (4 in.) over st.st. on No. 8 (4 mm) needles.

ABBREVIATIONS
k., knit; **p.**, purl; **st.st.**, stocking stitch; **cm.**, centimetres; **in.**, inches; **rep.**, repeat; **rem.**, remaining; **foll.**, following; **beg.**, beginning; **alt.**, alternate; **inc.**, increase; **dec.**, decrease; **sts.**, stitches; **patt.**, pattern; **w.s.**, wrong side; **r.s.**, right side; **cont.**, continue.

FRONT
**With No. 10 (3¼ mm) needles, cast on 94 (102; 110; 118) sts. and work in rib as follows:
1st row: *K. 2, p. 2, rep. from * to last 2 sts., k. 2.
2nd row: *P. 2, k. 2, rep. from * to last 2 sts., p. 2.
Rep. these 2 rows to form rib and work straight in rib as set until piece measures 5 cm. (2 in.) from beg., ending w.s. row.
Change to No. 8 (4 mm) needles and st.st. (*1st row:* K., *2nd row:* P.) and dec. 1 st. at each end of every 8th (8th; 10th; 10th) row 4 times in all.
Work straight in st.st. on these rem. 86 (94; 102; 110) sts. until piece measures 18 (19; 20; 21) cm. 7 (7½; 7¾; 8) in. from beg., ending w.s. row. **
Cont. in st.st. as set and inc. 1 st. at each end of every foll. 18th (18th; 20th; 20th) row 3 times in all, until 92 (100; 108; 116) sts. are on needle.
Work straight in st.st. on these sts. until piece measures 38 (39; 40; 41) cm. 15 (15¼; 15¾; 16) in. from beg. ending w.s. row.
Cast off 4 sts. at beg. of next 2 rows, 3 sts. at start of foll. 2 rows and 2 sts. at beg. of next 2 rows.
Dec. 1 st. at each end of next and every foll. alt. row 4 times in all.
Work straight in st.st. on these rem. 66 (74; 82; 90) sts. until piece measures 55 (57; 59; 61) cm. 21½ (22; 23; 24) in. from beg. ending w.s. row.
Next row: K. 25 (28; 31; 34) sts., leave next 16 (18; 20; 22) sts. on spare pin, then k. to end.
Now cont. in st.st. on these last sts. only and p. 1 row.
Next row: Cast off 2 sts. then k. to end.
P. 1 row.
Rep. these last 2 rows 5 more times.
Cast off rem. 13 (16; 19; 22) sts.
Rejoin yarn to neck edge of rem. sts. and complete to match first side, reversing all shapings.

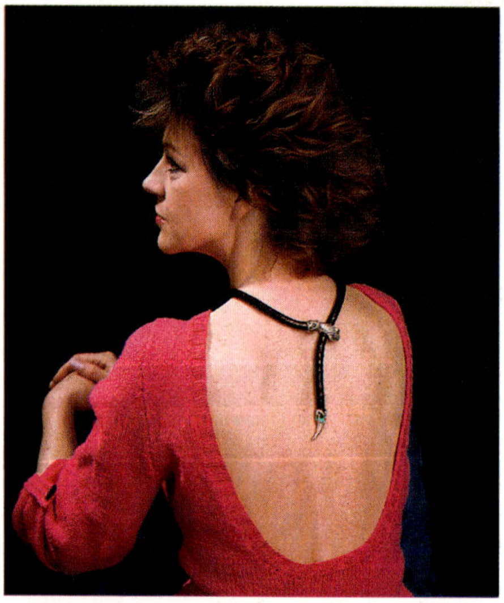

BACK
Work as for front from ** to **.
Continue in st.st. for a further 14 rows.
Next row: K 33 (37; 41; 45) sts., leave next 20 sts. on a spare pin, then k. to end.
Work 2 rows on these last sts. only.
Now cont. in st.st. on these last sts. only and inc. at side edge on next and 2 foll. 18th rows, and *at the same time* cont. as folls.:
Cast off 2 sts. at beg. of foll. alt. row.
P. 1 row.
Cast off 2 sts. at beg. of next row, then k. to end and p. 1 row.
Dec. 1 st. at beg. of next and every foll. alt. row 3 times in all, then p. 1 row.
Still inc. at side edge as set, dec. 1 st. at neck edge on next and every foll. 18th row until piece measures 38 (39; 40; 41) cm. 15 (15¼; 15¾; 16) in. from beg. ending r.s. row.
Dec. at armhole edge as for front, and keep neck edges dec's. correct until 5 (6; 7; 8) have been worked at neck edge and underarm shaping has been completed.
Work straight in st.st. on these rem. 13 (16; 19; 22) sts. until back matches front to shoulder, ending w.s. row.
Cast off.
Rejoin yarn to neck edge of rem. sts. and complete to match first side, reversing all shapings.

SLEEVES
With No. 8 (4 mm) needles, cast on 70 (72; 74; 77) sts. and work in st.st. until sleeve measures 44 (45; 46; 47) cm. 17 (17½; 18; 18½) in. from beg., ending w.s. row.
Cast off 4 sts. at beg. of next 2 rows, 3 sts. at start of foll. 2 rows and 2 sts. at beg. of next 2 rows.
Dec. 1 st. at each end of next and every foll. 3rd row, until 24 (24; 24; 25) sts. rem., ending w.s. row.
Cast off 2 sts. at beg. of next 2 rows and 3 sts. at beg. of foll. 2 rows.
Cast off rem. 14 (14; 14; 15) sts.
Work a further piece to match.

TAB
With No. 10 (3¼ mm) needles, cast on 10 sts. and work in rib as for welts for 12 cm. (5 in.), ending w.s. row.
Next row: Rib 4, cast off 2 sts. rib to end.

Next row: Rib as set, casting on 2 sts. over those cast off on previous row.
Rib 1 row, then cast off ribwise.
Work a further piece to match.

NECK EDGINGS

Join R. shoulder seam. With r.s. of work facing, and No. 10 (3¼ mm) needles pick up and k. 18 sts. from side front neck, then k. 16 (18; 20; 22) sts. from pins at front neck edge, then pick up and k. 18 sts. from side front neck, then pick up and k. 81 (84; 89; 92) sts. from side back neck edge, then k. across 20 sts. from pin at centre back, then pick up and k. 81 (84; 89; 92) sts. from rem. side back neck edge. 234 (242; 254; 262) sts.
Change to rib as follows:
1st row: P. 3, * k. 2, p. 2, rep. from * to last 3 sts., k. 3.
2nd row: As 1st row.
Rep. these 2 rows to form rib and work straight until piece measures 2.5 cm. (1 in.) from beg., ending w.s. row.
Cast off ribwise.

TO MAKE UP

Join rem. shoulder seam, cont. across neck edgings. Sew in sleeves, then join side and sleeve seams. Roll back sleeves to elbow, making a cuff 6 cm. (2 in.) wide, showing the w.s. of fabric. Sew tab around cuff by placing the end without the buttonhole under the cuff on the w.s. of sleeve, opposite the sleeve seam, and sewing through single thickness above the cuff to sew on button on r.s. of work. Fasten tab around cuff to button on r.s. of work. Rep. for other side. Do not press. Darn in loose ends.

Patrick Hughes
STAR-STUDDED SWEATER

Patrick Hughes, the painter, has almost made rainbows his trademark. One of his paintings hangs in London's Tate Gallery and Christie's limited edition Hughes prints can be bought by discerning collectors. Now he has turned to painting the stars. If you want to look like a star and don't have Patrick's deft touch with a paintbrush, how about using a couple of deft knitting needles to make this star studded sweater?

MATERIALS					
Patons Clansman DK (**M**)	**50 g. balls**	11	12	12	13
(**C**)	**50 g. balls**	1	1	1	1
Pair each No. 10 (3¼ mm) and No. 8 (4 mm) knitting needles.					
Shoulder pads.					
MEASUREMENTS					
To fit chest	**cm.**	97	102	107	112
	in.	38	40	42	44
Length	**cm.**	64	65	66	67
	in.	25	25½	26	26
Sleeve seam	**cm.**	46	47	47	48
	in.	18	18½	18½	19

TENSION
22 sts. and 30 rows to 10 cm. (4 in.) measured over st.st. on No. 8 (4 mm) needles.

ABBREVIATIONS
k., knit; **p.**, purl; **st.**, stitch; **tog.**, together; **dec.**, decrease; **beg.**, beginning; **alt.**, alternate; **rep.**, repeat; **patt.**, pattern; **cont.**, continue; **foll.**, following; **rem.**, remaining; **r.s.**, right side; **w.s.**, wrong side; **cm.**, centimetres; **mm.**, millimetres; **in.**, inches; **MS.**, Main Shade; **C.**, Contrast; **m.1**, make 1 stitch by picking up horizontal loop lying before next stitch and working into back of it.

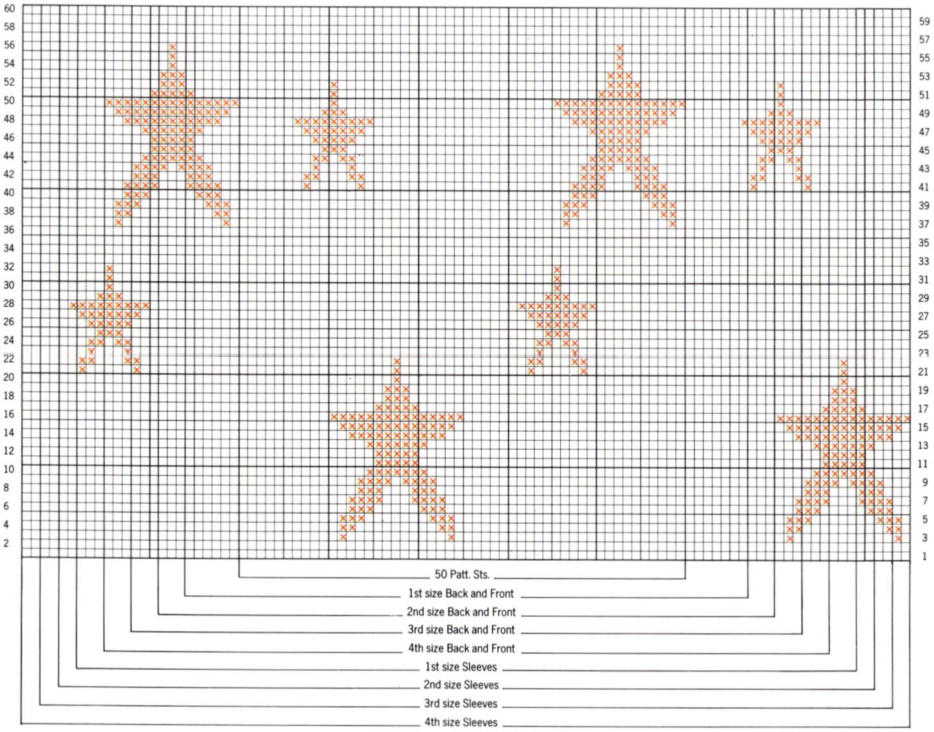

MOTIF KNITTING NOTE
When working in patt. from chart, do not carry C. across back of work, use separate balls of yarn as required, twisting yarns on w.s. to avoid a hole.
Do not work part of stars only whole stars.
Read odd rows k. from right to left and even rows p. from left to right.

BACK
**With No. 10 (3¼ mm) needles and MS, cast on 100 (106; 112; 118) sts. and work in k. 1, p. 1 rib for 9 cm. (3½ in.).
Next row: Rib 2 (5; 2; 5), m.1, [rib 8 (8; 9; 9), m.1] 12 times, rib 2 (5; 2; 5).
[113 (119; 125; 131) sts.]
Change to No. 8 (4 mm) needles and joining in and breaking of yarns as required, work in patt. from chart, rep. the 50 patt. sts. twice and working end sts. as indicated.
Work straight until back measures 37 cm. (14½ in.) ending with r.s. facing.
Shape armholes, keeping patt. correct, by casting off 4 (4; 5; 5) sts. at beg. of next 2 rows.
Dec. 1 st. at each end of next 3 (3; 5; 5) rows.
Work 1 row.
Now dec. 1 st. at each end of next and every foll. alt. row until 87 (91; 95; 99) sts. rem.**
Work straight until armhole measures 27 (28; 29; 30) cm. 10½ (11; 11½; 12) in. ending with r.s. facing.
Shape shoulders by casting off 8 (8; 9; 9) sts. at beg. of next 4 rows, then 8 (9; 8; 9) sts. at beg. of

foll. 2 rows.
Leave rem. 39 (41; 43; 45) sts. on a spare needle.

FRONT
Work as for back from ** to **.
Work straight until armhole measures 19 (20; 20; 21) cm. 7½ (8; 8; 8) in. ending with r.s. facing.
Divide for neck, keeping patt. correct, as folls.:
Next row: Patt. 32 (33; 34; 35) sts. k. 2 tog., turn and leave rem. sts. on a spare needle.
Dec. 1 st. at neck edge on every row until 24 (25; 26; 27) sts. rem.
Work a few rows straight until front matches back to shoulder, ending with r.s. facing.
Shape shoulder by casting off 8 (8; 9; 9) sts. at beg. of next and foll. alt row.
Work 1 row. Cast off rem. 8 (9; 8; 9) sts.
With r.s. facing, slip centre 19 (21; 23; 25) sts. on a length of yarn, rejoin yarn to rem. sts. k. 2 tog., patt. to end.
Work to match first side, reversing shapings.

SLEEVES
With No. 10 (3¼ mm) needles and MS., cast on 50 (52; 54; 56) sts. and work in k. 1, p. 1, rib for 8 cm. (3 in.).
Next row: [Rib 1, m.1] 13 (14; 15; 16) times, [rib 2, m.1] 12 times, [rib 1, m.1] 12 (13; 14; 15) times, rib 1. [87 (91; 95; 99) sts.].
Change to No. 8 (4 mm) needles and joining in and breaking off yarns as required, work in patt. from chart, rep. the 50 patt. sts. once and working end sts. as indicated, until sleeve measures 46 (47; 47; 48) cm. 18 (18½; 18½; 19) in. ending with r.s. facing.
Shape top, keeping patt. correct, by casting off 4 (4; 5; 5) sts. at beg. of next 2 rows.
Dec. 1 st. at each end of next row. Work 3 rows.
Rep. last 4 rows 2 (1; 1; 1) times more.
Now dec. 1 st. at each end of next and every foll. alt. row until 23 sts. rem., ending with r.s. facing.
Cast off rem. sts.

MAKE UP AND NECK BORDER
With wrong side or work facing, press parts lightly, omitting ribbing and following instructions on the ball band. Join right shoulder seam.

NECK BORDER
With r.s. facing, No. 10 (3¼ mm) needles and MS, knit up 18 (18; 20; 20) sts. down left side of neck, k. 19 (21; 23; 25) sts. from front, knit up 18 (18; 20; 20) sts. up right side of neck, k. 39 (41; 43; 45) sts. from back. [94 (98; 106; 110) sts.]
Work in k. 1, p.1 rib for 6 cm. (2 in.).
Using a No. 8 (4 mm) needle, cast off loosely in rib.
Join left shoulder and neck border.
Fold neck border in half to w.s. and slip hem in position.
Join side and sleeve seams.
Insert sleeves.
Sew in shoulder pads.

Kiki Dee

COLOUR CO-ORDINATED HIT NUMBER

Don't break your heart over this little wrap style coat, sweater and skirt. Just get out the needles and run them up for yourself. Pop singer Kiki swears it's her favourite cover-up. After a super, successful stint in the musical *Pump Boys and Dinettes* Kiki is now busy developing her studio work.

MATERIALS

Wrap Style Coat					
Patons Diploma DK	**50 g. balls**	24	26		
Sweater					
Patons Diploma DK	**50 g. balls**	11	12		
Skirt					
Patons Diploma DK	**50 g. balls**	10	10	11	11

Pair each Nos. 9 (3¾ mm) and 8 (4 mm) knitting needles.
A circular No. 8 (4 mm) needle maybe useful for either wrap or sweater.

MEASUREMENTS

Wrap style coat					
To fit bust	**cm.**	81–86	91–97		
	in.	32–34	36–38		
Length	**cm.**	90	90		
	in.	35½	35½		
Sweater					
To fit bust	**cm.**	81–86	91–97		
	in.	32–34	36–38		
Length	**cm.**	40	40		
	in.	16½	16½		
Sleeve seam	**cm.**	38	38		
	in.	15	15		
Skirt					
To fit hips	**cm.**	86	91	97	102
	in.	34	36	38	40
Length	**cm.**	70	70	70	70
	in.	27½	27½	27½	27½

TENSION
30 sts. and 32 rows to 10 cm. measured over pattern on No. 8 (4 mm) needles.

ABBREVIATIONS
k., knit; **p.**, purl; **sts.**, stitches; **tog.**, together; **inc.**, increase; **dec.**, decrease; **beg.**, beginning; **rep.**, repeat; **patt.**, pattern; **cont.**, continue; **foll.**, following; **rem.**, remaining; **r.s.**, right side; **w.s.**, wrong side; **cm.**, centimetres; **mm.**, millimetres; **in.**, inches.

WRAP STYLE COAT
Worked in one piece from lower edge back to lower edges front.
With No. 9 (3¾ mm) needles, cast on 272 (305) sts. and work in rib as follows:
1st row: * K. 2, p. 1; rep. from * to last 2 sts., k. 2.
2nd row: * P. 2, k. 1; rep. from * to last 2 sts., p. 2.
These 2 rows form rib.
Work in rib for 5 cm. (2 in.), ending with 2nd row.
Change to No. 8 (4 mm) needles and work in patt. as follows:
1st row: K. 2, * p. 1, k. 2; rep. from * to end.
2nd row: K. 1, p. 1, * k. 2, p. 1; rep. from * to end.
These 2 rows form patt.
Work straight in patt. until back measures 90 cm. (35½ in.), ending with r.s. facing.
Place markers at each end of last row – these mark shoulders.
Divide for fronts, keeping patt. correct, as follows:
Next row: Patt. 106 (120) sts., cast off centre 60 (65) sts., now cast on 31 (32) sts. for front, patt. across 137 (152) sts. for left front.
Cont. in patt. until work measures 85 cm. (33½ in.) from marker, ending with r.s. facing.
Change to No. 9 (3¾ mm) needles and work in rib, as given for lower edge on back, for 5 cm. (2 in.), ending with 2nd row.
Cast off.
With w.s. facing, rejoin yarn to sts. for right front, cast on 31 (32) sts., patt. across all 137 (152) sts. for right front.
Work to match left front.
Do not press.

SWEATER
Knitted sideways from sleeve to sleeve.
With No.9 (3¾ mm) needles, cast on 134 (146) sts. and work in rib as follows:
1st row: K. 2, * p. 1, k. 2; rep. from * to end.
2nd row: P. 2, * k. 1, p. 2; rep. from * to end.
These 2 rows form rib.
Work in rib for 4 cm. (1½ in.), ending with 2nd row.
Change to No. 8 (4 mm) needles and work in patt. as follows:
1st row: K. 2, * p. 1, k. 2; rep. from * to end.
2nd row: K. 1, p. 1, * k. 2, p. 1; rep. from * to end.
These 2 rows form patt.
Work straight until sleeve measures 38 cm. (15 in.), ending with r.s. facing.
Cast on 54 (48) sts. at beg. of next 2 rows. 242 sts.
Work 34 (38) more rows in patt. across all sts.
Divide for neck, keeping patt. correct, as follows:
Next row: Patt. 113 sts., cast off 12 sts., patt. to end.
Cont. on last group of sts. for back.
Dec. 1 st. at neck edge on next 8 rows. 109 sts.
Work straight for 58 (66) rows, thus ending with w.s. facing.
Now inc. 1 st. at neck edge on next 8 rows.
Patt. 1 row, turn and cast on 4 sts., leave all 121 sts. on a spare needle.
With w.s. facing, rejoin yarn to sts. for front, dec. 1 st. at neck edge on next 14 rows. 99 sts.
Work straight for 45 (53) rows, thus ending with r.s. facing.
Now inc. 1 st. at neck edge on next 14 rows.
Patt. 1 row.
Cast on 8 sts., patt. to end. 121 sts.
Join work together again as follows:
Next row: Patt. across 121 sts. from front, patt. across 121 sts. from back. 242 sts.
Work 35 (39) rows in patt. across all sts.
Cast off 54 (48) sts. at beg. of next 2 rows. 134 (146) sts.
Work straight until sleeve measures 34 cm. (13 in.), ending with r.s. facing.
Change to No. 9 (3¼ mm) needles and work in rib as given for other sleeve edge, for 4 cm. (1½ in.), ending with r.s. facing. Cast off.

MAKE UP AND NECK BORDER
Do not press.
Neck Border
With No. 9 (3¾ mm) needles, cast on 7 sts. and work in rib as follows:
1st row: K. 2, (k. 1, p. 1) twice, k. 1.
2nd row: K. 1, (p. 1, k. 1) 3 times.
Rep. these 2 rows until border fits around neck edge. Stitch in postition as you go along.
Join side and underarm seams.

SKIRT
Work 4 pieces the same.
With No. 9 (3¾ mm) needles, cast on 68 (74; 77; 80) sts. and work in rib as follows:
1st row: K. 2, * p. 1, k. 2; rep. from * to end.
2nd row: P. 2, * k. 1, p. 2; rep. from * to end.
These 2 rows form rib.
Work in rib for 2 cm. (¾ in.), ending with 2nd row.
Change to No. 8 (4 mm) needles and work in patt. as follows:
1st row: K. 2, * p. 1, k. 2; rep. from * to end.
2nd row: K. 1, p. 1, * k. 2, p. 1; rep. from * to end.
These 2 rows form patt.
Work straight in patt. until work measures 47 cm. (18½ in.), ending with r.s. facing.
Shape sides by dec. 1 st. at each end of next and every foll. 10th row until 56 (62, 65, 68) sts. rem.
Work straight until piece measures 70 cm. (27½ in.), from beg., ending with r.s. facing.
Change to No. 9 (3¾ mm) needles and work in rib, as given for lower edge, for 5 cm. (2 in.), ending with r.s. facing. Cast off.

TO MAKE UP
Do not press.
Centre front and centre back seams are worked as a feature to r.s., side seams are worked to w.s. as normal. Join seams.
Fold waist ribbing in half to w.s. and slip stitch in position, leaving an opening for elastic.
Insert elastic and adjust to fit waist, join elastic and close opening.

Tim Pigott-Smith
TRIPLE SLEEVE LINEN-LOOK

Tim Pigott-Smith won the Best Actor of the Year Award for his performance as Captain Ronald Merrick in *Jewel in the Crown.* A gentler sort of chap in real life, he took great care in designing this original and flattering sweater with a three-way sleeve. It can be taken to pieces in the very hottest weather and then, as day cools into night, bits can be added back.

MATERIALS

Patons Linen Look	**50 g. balls**	11	12	12	13

Pair each needles Nos. 10 (3¼ mm) and 8 (4 mm).
2.32 metres (7½ ft.) of 2 cm. (¾ in.) wide matching or contrasting popper tape.
Matching thread.

MEASUREMENTS

To fit chest	**cm.**	91	97	102	107
	in.	36	38	40	42
Actual size	**cm.**	101	107	112	117
	in.	39½	42	44	46
Length from shoulder	**cm.**	69	70	71	73
	in.	27	27½	28	28½
Length sleeve seam	**cm.**	48	48	49	49
	in.	19	19	19½	19½

TENSION
21 sts. and 29 rows are equal to 10 cm. (4 in.) square measured over st.st. and worked on No. 8 (4 mm) needles.

ABBREVIATIONS
k., knit; **p.**, purl; **sts.**, stitches; **st. st.**, stocking-stitch; **inc.**, increase; **cm.**, centimetres; **in.**, inches.

To work larger sizes follow figures shown between the brackets. Where only one set of figures, this applies to all sizes.

BACK AND FRONT (both alike)
Using No. 10 (3¼ mm) needles cast on 102 (108; 114; 118) sts. and work in k. 1, p. 1 rib until rib measures 7.5 cm. (3 in.) from cast on edge. Inc. 6 (6; 6; 8) sts. evenly across last row (108 (114; 120; 126) sts. in all).
Change to No. 8 (4 mm) needles and proceed to work in st.st. (first row *purl*, this is the right side of sweater) until work measures 41 (42; 43; 43) cm. 16 (16½; 17; 17) in. from cast on edge, tie coloured markers at each end of this row for armholes. Continue to work in st.st. as before until work measures 65 (66; 67; 69) cm. 25½ (26; 26½; 27) in. from cast on edge.

SHAPE NECK (with right side facing).
Still using No. 8 (4 mm) needles now work in k. 1, p. 1 rib until work measures 69 (70; 71; 73) cm. 27 (27½; 28; 29) in. With right side facing, cast off in rib.

SLEEVES
Lower Sleeve
Using No. 10 (3¼ mm) needles cast on 44 (44; 48; 48) sts. and work in k. 1, p. 1 rib until rib measures 5 cm. (2 in.) from cast on edge. Inc. 48 (48; 44; 44) sts. evenly across last row. (92 sts. in all).
Change to No. 8 (4 mm) needles and proceed to work in st.st. (first row *purl* this is the right side of sleeve). Inc. one st. at each end of next 3rd and then every following 4th row until there are 120 sts. on the needle. Continue on these sts. until work measures 29 cm. (11½ in.) from cast on edge. With right side facing cast off.

Upper Sleeve
Using No. 8 (4 mm) needles cast on 120 sts. and proceed to work in st.st. (first row *purl*, this is the right side of sleeve) until work measures 19 (19; 20; 20) cm. 7½ (7½; 8; 8) in. from cast on edge. With right side facing, cast off.

TO MAKE UP
Do not press. Join both shoulder seams 12.75 (14.25; 15.5; 16.75) cm. 5(5¾; 6; 6½) in. in from shoulder. Cut the popper-tape into 4 pieces. Turn all ends. Stitch bottom side of popper-tape to top edge of lower sleeve.
Stitch top side of popper tape to lower edge of upper sleeve.
Stitch bottom side of popper tape to sleeve head.
Stitch top side of popper tape to sweater between coloured armhole markers.
Join side seams to popper tape.
Join sleeve seams rib to tape on lower sleeve and tape to tape on upper sleeve so that it is possible to undo each section.

Kate Garner

TOP OF THE POPS BLACK MINI DRESS

Kate Garner, lead singer of the pop group Haysi Fantayzee, has almost as much style as her close friend Boy George. Enter the style wars on her side in this black mini-dress with its dramatic halter neck for maximum impact.

MATERIALS

Dress				
Patons Cotton Perle	**50 g. balls**	8	9	10
Armwarmers				
Patons Cotton Perle	**50 g. balls**	1	1	1

Pair each Nos. 10 (3¼ mm) and 8 (4 mm) needles.
Set of 4 No. 10 (3¼ mm) needles, pointed both ends.
No. 11 (3.00 mm) crochet hook. 6 buttons
10 cm. (4 in.) buckle.

MEASUREMENTS

To fit bust	**cm.**	81	86	91
	in.	32	34	36
To fit hips	**cm.**	86	91	97
	in.	34	36	38
length from top of shoulders	**cm.**	76	80	82
	in.	30	31½	32½

TENSION
22 sts. and 29 rows measured over 10 cm. (4 in.) of stocking stitch on No. 8 (4 mm) needles.

ABBREVIATIONS
k., knit; **p.**, purl; **sts.** stitches; **st.st.**, stocking st.; **g.st.**, garter st.; **mm.**, millimetres; **cm.**, centimetres; **in.**, inches; **dec.**, decrease by working 2 sts. together; **m.1**, pick up horizontal loop lying before next st. and work into back of it; **sl.**, slip; **p.s.s.o.**, pass the slipped st. over; **tog.**, together; **rep.**, repeat; **beg.**, beginning; **d.c.**, double crochet.

BACK
**With No. 10 (3¼ mm) needles, cast on 91 (97; 103) sts. and work 5 rows g.st., ie. every row knit.
Next row: K. 8 (8; 9), m.1, *k. 15 (16; 17), m.1; rep. from * to last 8 (9; 9) sts., k. 8 (9;9). 97 (103; 109); sts.
Change to No. 8 (4 mm) needles and st.st., starting with a p. row, and work straight until back measures 7 (10; 13) cm. 3 (4; 5) in. at centre from start, ending with a p. row.
Shape skirt as follows:
Next row: K. 17 (18; 19), sl. 1, k. 1, p.s.s.o., k. 59 (63; 67), k. 2 tog., k. 17 (18; 19).95 (101; 107) sts. Work 7 rows straight.
Next row: K. 17 (18; 19), sl. 1, k. 1, p.s.s.o., k. 57 (61; 65), k. 2 tog., k. 17 (18; 19).93 (99; 105) sts. Work 7 rows straight.
Continue dec. 2 sts. thus on next and every following 8th row until 77 (83; 89) sts. remain.
Work 15 rows straight.
Next row: K. 17 (18; 19), m.1, k. to last 17 (18; 19) sts., m.1, k. 17 (18; 19).79 (85; 91) sts. Work 7 rows straight. Rep. last 8 rows until there are 91 (97; 103) sts.
Work straight until back measures 58 (61; 63) cm. 23 (24; 25) in. at centre from start, ending with right side facing.
Shape armholes by casting off 6 sts. at beg. of next 2 rows, then dec. 1 st. at each end of every row until 55 (61; 67) sts. remain, then on next and every alternate row until 45 (49; 53) sts. remain. Work 1 row straight.**
Divide for back opening as follows:
Next row: K. 2 tog., k. 20 (22; 24), turn and leave remaining sts. on a spare needle.
Continue on these 21 (23; 25) sts. for first side and work 1 row straight, then dec. 1 st. at armhole edge on next and every alternate row as before until 18 (20; 22) sts. remain.
Work straight until back measures 76 (80; 82) cm. 30 (31½; 32½) in. at centre from start, ending with right side facing.
Shape shoulder by casting off 3 (4; 5) sts. at beg. of next row, work 1 row straight. Leave remaining 15 (16; 17) sts. on 1 spare needle.
With right side facing, rejoin yarn to remaining sts., cast off centre st., k. to last 2 sts., k. 2 tog. Finish to correspond with first side.

FRONT
Work as for back from ** to **. Continue dec. at each end of next and every alternate row until 37 (41; 45) sts. remain. Work straight until front measures 71 (75; 77) cm. 28 (29½; 30½) in. at centre from start, ending with a p. row.
Here divide for neck.
Next row: K. 11 (12; 13), turn and leave remaining sts. on a spare needle.
Continue on these 11 (12; 13) sts. for first side, dec. 1 st. at neck edge on every row until 3 (4, 5) sts. remain.
Work a few rows straight until front matches back at armhole edge, ending with right side facing. Cast off.
With right side facing, slip centre 15 (17; 19) sts. on a spare needle, rejoin yarn to remaining sts., k. to end. Finish to correspond with first side.

COLLAR
Join shoulder seams.
With right side facing and using the set of No. 10 (3¼ mm) needles, start at left side of back opening and k. 15 (16; 17) from left side of back, pick up and k. 17 down left side of neck, k. 15 (17; 19) from centre, pick up and k. 17 up right side, then k. 15 (16; 17) from right side of back. 79 (83; 87) sts.
Arrange sts. evenly on 3 needles and starting with a p. row, work backwards and forwards with a 4th for 23 rows.
Next row: Purl. The last row forms folding ridge for collar.
Work a further 22 rows st.st., starting with a p. row. Cast off purlways.

ARMHOLE BORDERS
With right side facing and No. 10 (3¼ mm) needles, pick up and k. 100 (108; 108) sts. round each armhole and work 5 rows k. 1, p. 1 rib. Cast off evenly in rib.

BELT

Right side
**With No. 8 (4 mm) needles, cast on 44 sts.
1st row: Knit.
2nd row: K. 3, p. to last 3 sts., k. 3.
Rep. last 2 rows once more.
Shape as follows:
Next row: K. 3, sl. 1, k. 1, p.s.s.o., k. to last 5 sts., k. 2 tog., k. 3.
Work 5 rows straight.
Rep. last 6 rows until 26 sts. remain.**
Work straight until belt measures 24 (25; 27) cm. 9½ (10; 10½) in. at centre from start, ending with right side facing. Cast off.

Left side
Work as for right side from ** to **.
Work straight until belt measures 32 (34; 37) cm. 12½ (13½; 14½) in. at centre from start, ending with right side facing.
Shape mitred end as follows:
Next row: K. to last 5 sts., k. 2 tog., k. 3.
Next row: K. 3, p. to last 3 sts., k. 3.
Rep. last 2 rows until 7 sts. remain, ending with right side facing.
Next row: K. 3, k. 2 tog., k. 2.
Next row: Knit.
Next row: K. 2, k. 2 tog., k. 2.
Next row: Knit.
Next row: K. 2, k. 2 tog., k. 1.
Next row: Knit.
Next row: K. 1, k. 2 tog., k. 1.
Next row: Knit.
Next row: K. 2 tog., k. 1.
Next row: K. 2, turn. k. 2 tog. and fasten off.

TO MAKE UP
Do not press.
Fold collar in half at the purl ridge, purl at side inside and slip-hem lightly in position all round.
Using crochet hook, work in d.c. along collar and back opening. Work back in d.c., making 6 buttonloops evenly spaced along right edge. To make a buttonloop: make 3 ch., miss 2 d.c. Work a further row in d.c., working 3 d.c. into each buttonloop. Fasten off.
Attach buckle to right belt piece, then pin wide edge of piece to right side seam on back, top of belt to come 51 (52; 53) cm. 20 (20½; 21) in. down from shoulder.
Pin left belt piece to correspond on left side seam, then join side seams, catching belt in seam as you do so. Sew on buttons.

ARMWARMERS (2)
With No. 10 (3¼ mm) needles, cast on 46 sts. and work in k. 1, p. 1 rib for 14 cm. (5½ in.). Cast off evenly in rib. Join side edges.

Julie Walters

DIAMOND PATTERN SWEATER

Funny, adorable Julie Walters may have favoured tarty clothes in *Educating Rita,* but in real life she prefers easy to wear trousers and sweaters – something comfortable to throw on and yet still look smart enough to face her always busy day.

MATERIALS

Patons Beehive Chunky	**(MS)**	**50 g. balls**	4	5
Patons Beehive Chunky	**(L)**	**50 g. balls**	3	3
Patons Beehive Chunky	**(D)**	**50 g. balls**	3	3
Patons Siberia	**(S)**	**50 g. balls**	2	3
Patons Cotton Ribbon	**(C)**	**50 g. balls**	3	3

Pair each Nos. 4 (6 mm) and 6 (5 mm) needles.

MEASUREMENTS

To fit bust	**cm.**	81–86	91–97
	in.	32–34	36–38
Length from top of shoulders	**cm.**	60–61	60–61
	in.	23½–24	23½–24
Sleeve seam	**cm.**	42	42
	in.	16½	16½

TENSION

Pattern is based on a standard stocking stitch tension of 15 sts. and 20 rows measured over 10 cm. (4 in.) of Beehive Chunky on No. 4 (6 mm) needles.

ABBREVIATIONS

k., knit; **p.**, purl; **sts.**, stitches; **st.st.**, stocking st.; **rev.st.st.**, reversed stocking st.; **mm.**, millimetres; **cm.**, centimetres; **in.**, inches; **rep.**, repeat; **m.1**, pick up horizontal loop lying before next st. and work into back of it; **patt.**, pattern; **dec.**, decrease by working 2 sts. together; **beg.**, beginning; **tog.**, together; **MS**, Main Shade; **L**, 1st Contrast Shade; **D**, 2nd Contrast Shade; **S**, 3rd Contrast Shade; **C**, 4th Contrast Shade.

BACK

With No. 6 (5 mm) needles and MS, cast on 61 (65) sts.

1st row: Right side facing, k. 1, * p. 1, k. 1; rep. from * to end.

2nd row: P. 1, * k. 1, p. 1; rep. from * to end.

Rep. last 2 rows until work measures 7 cm. (3 in.) at centre, ending with 1st row.

Next row: Rib 3 (5), m.1, * rib 3, m.1; rep. from * to last 4 (6) sts., rib 4 (6). 80 (84) sts.

Change to No. 4 (6 mm) needles and joining in colours as required, work in patt. as follows:

1st row: Right side facing, k., 1 (3) L, 14 S, 2 MS, 14 L, 2 C, 14 MS, 2 D, 14 C, 2 S, 14 D, 1 (3) L.

N.B.: Twist yarns on wrong side of work when changing colour to avoid a hole.

2nd row: K. 1 (3) L, p. 14 D, k. 2 S, p. 14 C, k. 2 D, p. 14 MS, k. 2 C, p. 14 L, k. 2 MS, p. 14 S, k. 1 (3) L.

3rd row: P. 2 (4) L, k. 12 S, p. 4 MS, k. 12 L, p. 4 C, k. 12 MS, p. 4 D, k. 12 C, p. 4 S, k. 12 D, p. 2 (4) L.

4th and every following alternate row: As previous row, but reading 'k.' for 'p.' and 'p.' for 'k.' throughout.

5th row: P. 3 (5) L, k. 10 S, p. 6 MS, k. 10 L, p. 6 C, k. 10 MS, p. 6 D, k. 10 C, p. 6 S, k. 10 D, p. 3 (5) L.

7th row: P. 4 (6) L, k. 8 S, p. 8 MS, k. 8 L, p. 8 C, k. 8 MS, p. 8 D, k. 8 C, p. 8 S, k. 8 D, p. 4 (6) L.

9th row: P. 5 (7) L, k. 6 S, p. 10 MS, k. 6 L, p. 10 C, k. 6 MS, p. 10 D, k. 6 C, p. 10 S, k. 6 D, p. 5 (7) L.

11th row: P. 6 (8) L, k. 4 S, p. 12 MS, k. 4 L, p. 12 C, k. 4 MS, p. 12 D, k. 4 C, p. 12 S, k. 4 D, p. 6 (8) L.

13th row: P. 7 (9) L, k. 2 S, p. 14 MS, k. 2 L, p. 14 C, k. 2 MS, p.14 D, k. 2 C, p. 14 S, k. 2 D, p. 7 (9) L.

15th row: P. 7 (9) L, k. 2 D, p. 14 MS, k. 2 S, p. 14 C, k. 2 L, p. 14 D, k. 2 MS, p. 14 S, k. 2 C, p. 7 (9) L.

17th row: P. 6 (8) L, k. 4 D, p. 12 MS, k. 4 S, p. 12 C, k. 4 L, p. 12 D, k. 4 MS, p. 12 S, k. 4 C, p. 6 (8) L.

19th row: P. 5 (7) L, k. 6 D, p. 10 MS, k. 6 S, p. 10 C, k. 6 L, p. 10 D, k. 6 MS, p. 10 S, k. 6 C, p 5 (7) L.

21st row: P. 4 (6) L, k. 8 D, p. 8 MS, k. 8 S, p. 8 C, k. 8 L, p. 8 D, k. 8 MS, p. 8 S, k. 8 C, p. 4 (6) L.

23rd row: P. 3 (5) L, k. 10 D, p. 6 MS, k. 10 S, p. 6 C, k. 10 L, p. 6 D, k. 10 MS, p. 6 S, k. 10 C, p. 3 (5) L.

25th row: P. 2 (4) L, k. 12 D, p. 4 MS, k. 12 S, p. 4 C, k. 12 L, p. 4 D, k. 12 MS, p. 4 S, k. 12 C, p. 2 (4) L.

27th row: P. 1 (3) L, k. 14 D, p. 2 MS, k. 14 S, p. 2 C, k. 14 L, p. 2 D, k. 14 MS, p. 2 S, k. 14 C, p. 1 (3) L.

28th row: As 4th. These 28 rows form diamond patt.

Continue thus in st.st. and rev.st.st. diamond patt. alternating colours by moving diamonds diagonally to the left each time. Your next 2 rows will read:

Next row: K., 1 (3) S, 14 D, 2 L, 14 S, 2 MS, 14 L, 2 C, 14 MS, 2 D, 14 C, 1 (3) S.

Next row: K. 1 (3) S, p. 14 C, k. 2 D, p. 14 MS, k. 2 C, p. 14 L, k. 2 MS, p. 14 S, k. 2 L, p. 14 D, k. 1 (3) S.

N.B.: When changing colour of rev.st.st. diamond the first row of the patt. must be worked knit instead of purl.

Work straight in patt. until back measures 34 cm. (13 ½ in.) at centre from start, ending with right side facing.

Continue in patt. shaping raglans by casting off 3 sts. at beg. of next 2 rows, then dec. 1 st. at each end of next and following 4th row. 70 (74) sts.

Work 3 rows straight, then dec. 1 st. at each end of next and every alternate row until 26 (28) sts. remain, ending with right side facing.

Leave sts. on a spare needle.

FRONT

Work as for back until 44 (46) sts. remain in raglan shaping, ending with right side facing. Here divide for neck.

Next row: Work 2 tog., patt. 14, turn and leave remaining sts. on a spare needle.

Continue on these 15 sts. for first side as follows:

Dec. 1 st. at neck edge on next and every alternate row and at the same time dec. 1 st. at raglan edge on every alternate row from last dec. until 6 sts. remain.

Now keep neck edge straight and continue dec. at raglan edge on alternate rows as before until 2 sts. remain.

Next row: Patt. 2, turn. Work 2 tog. and fasten off.

With right side facing, slip centre 12 (14) sts. on a spare needle, rejoin appropriate colours to remaining sts., patt. to last 2 sts., work 2 tog. Finish to correspond with first side.

SLEEVES

With No. 6 (5 mm) needles and MS, cast on 29 (31) sts. and work 7 cm. (3 in.) k. 1, p. 1 rib, as for back, ending with 1st row.

Next row: Rib 0 (1), * work into front and back of next st., m.1, (rib 1, m.1) 3 times; rep. from * to last 1 (2) sts., rib 1 (2). 64 (66) sts.

Change to No. 4 (6 mm) needles and work in patt. as for back, but working 4 instead of 5 diamond motifs. Your first 4 rows will read:

1st row: Right side facing, k., 7 (9) S, 2 MS, 14 L, 2 C, 14 MS, 2 D, 14 C, 2 S, 7 (9) D.

2nd row: P. 7 (9) D. k. 2 S, p. 14 C, k. 2 D, p. 14 MS, k. 2 C, p. 14 L, k. 2 MS, p. 7 (9) S.

3rd row: K. 6 (8) S, p. 4 MS, k. 12 L, p. 4 C, k. 12 MS, p. 4 D, k. 12 C, p. 4 S, k. 6 (8) D.

4th row: As 3rd, but reading 'p.' for 'k.' and 'k.' for 'p.' throughout.

Continue straight in diamond patt. thus, alternating colours as for back, until sleeve measures 42 cm. (16½ in.) at centre from start, ending with right side facing.

Continue in patt., shaping raglans by casting off 3 sts. at beg. of next 2 rows, then dec. 1 st. at each end of next 2 rows. 54 (56) sts.

Now dec. 1 st. at each end of next and every alternate row until 4 sts. remain, all sizes, ending with right side facing. Leave sts. on a spare needle.

NECK BORDER

Join raglan seams on right sleeve and front raglan seam on left sleeve.

With right side facing, No. 6 (5 mm) needles and MS, k. 4 from left sleeve, pick up and k. 16 sts. down left side of neck, k. 12 (14) from centre, pick up and k. 16 up right side, k. 4 from right sleeve, then k. 26 (28) from back. 78 (82) sts.

Work 6 cm. (2½ in.) k. 1, p. 1 rib. Cast off loosely in rib, using a bigger needle.

TO MAKE UP

Do not press. Join remaining raglan seam, then join neck border with a flat seam. Join side and sleeve seams, matching patt. carefully. Fold neck border in half to wrong side and slip-hem loosely in position all round.

KNITTING KNOW-HOW

When knitting know-how is in question, no book, no meticulous set of beginner's instructions, can substitute for the guidance of an experienced knitter. Fortunately there is usually someone nearby who will be prepared to give endless time and energy and best of all enthusiasm to your work. But, if there isn't, a few instructions are better than nothing. In the hope that we can be of some help, these instructions are intended to set you on your way.

NEEDLE CONVERSIONS

Metric	Imperial	USA
2mm	14	00
2¼mm	13	0
2¾mm	12	1
3mm	11	2
3¼mm	10	3
3¾mm	9	4
4mm	8	5
4½mm	7	6
5mm	6	7
5½mm	5	8
6mm	4	9
6½mm	3	10
7mm	2	10½
7½mm	1	11
8mm	0	12

HOLDING THE YARN

Twist the yarn or cotton around the little finger of your right hand or place it under the little finger, then over your third finger, under the second and over the index finger.

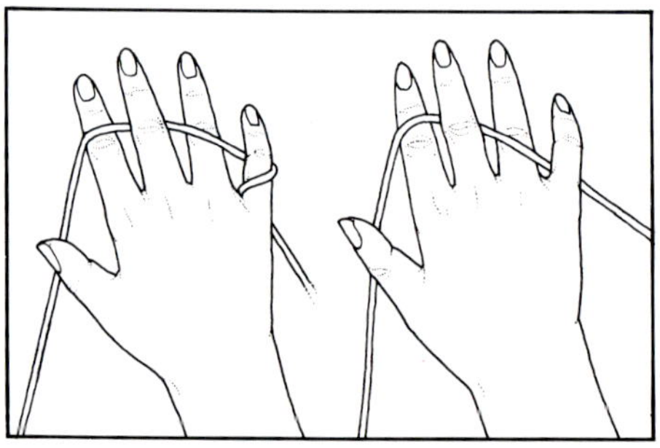

CASTING ON

1 Make a slip loop by winding the yarn twice around two fingers, then pull a loop through the twisted yarn with a knitting needle. Pull the yarn to tighten the slip loop. You now have your first stitch.

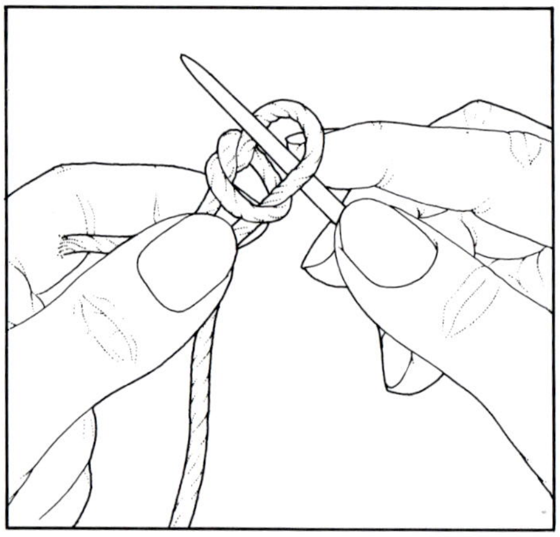

2 Take the needle with its single loop into your left hand. In your right hand take the second needle and slip it through the loop from front to back, so that the point rests just behind the point of the needle in your left hand.

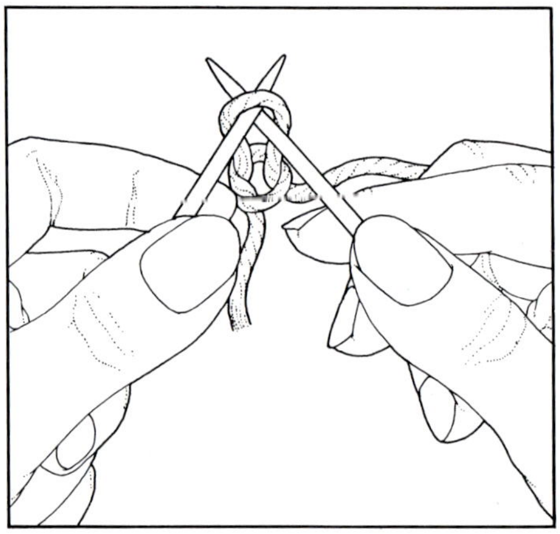

3 Twist the yarn under and over the right hand needle, holding the yarn well away from both needles to the right. Then slip your right needle with its single loop of yarn through the original slip loop.

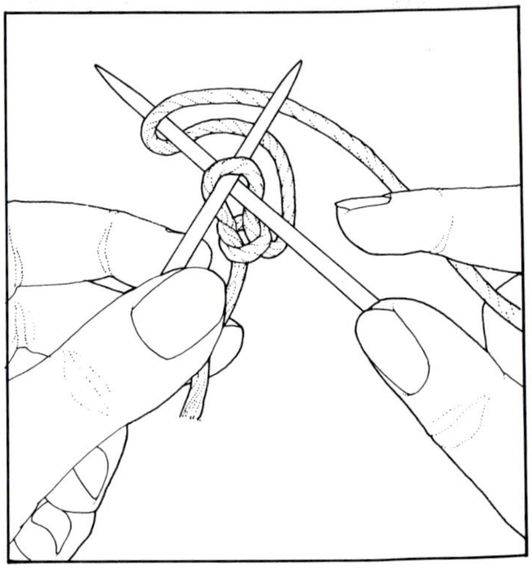

4 Now slip the stitch on your right hand needle onto the point of the left hand needle – still holding the yarn wound round your right hand as described.

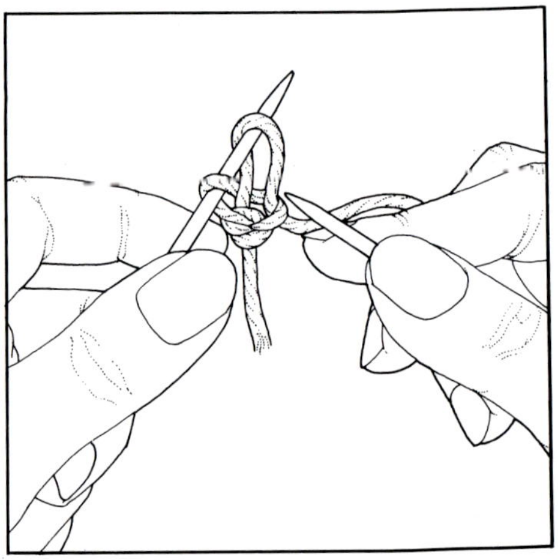

5 Repeat this until you have cast on all the stitches required.

KNIT AND PURL STITCHES

Knit and purl are the two basic ingredients of knitting. They make delightful patterns in combination. Once you have the hang of them any other stitch simply follows.

Knit Stitches

1 Hold the needle containing the cast on stitches in your left hand and pull the yarn to the back, behind the right hand needle. Do not let the yarn drift about as this will cause endless muddle and make the tension of your work irregular.

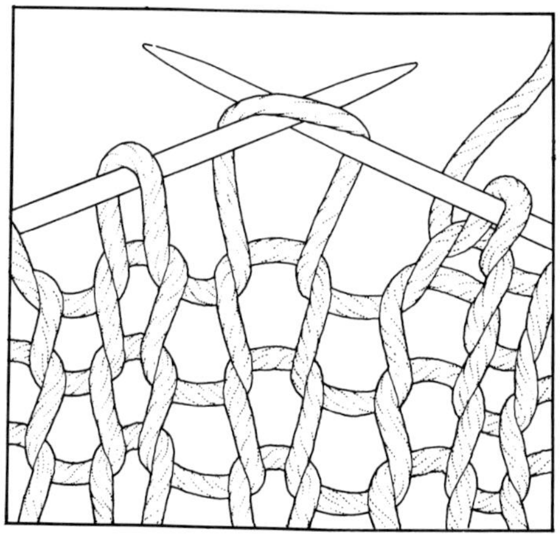

2 Now put the right hand needle through the back of the first stitch from right top left.

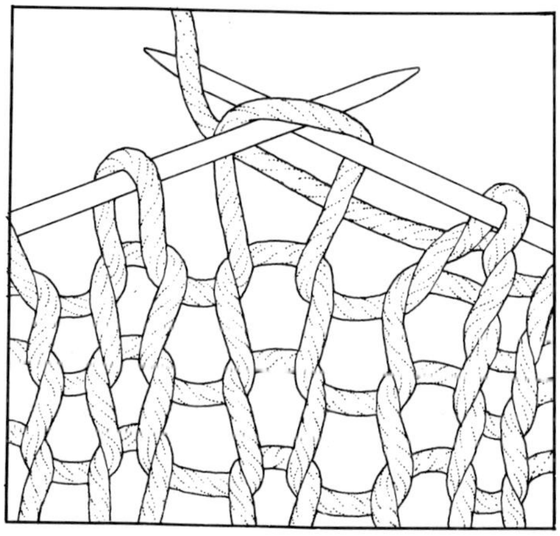

3 Take the yarn under and over the right hand needle. Then twist the right hand needle to pull the new loop through the old loop on the left hand needle and onto the right hand needle.

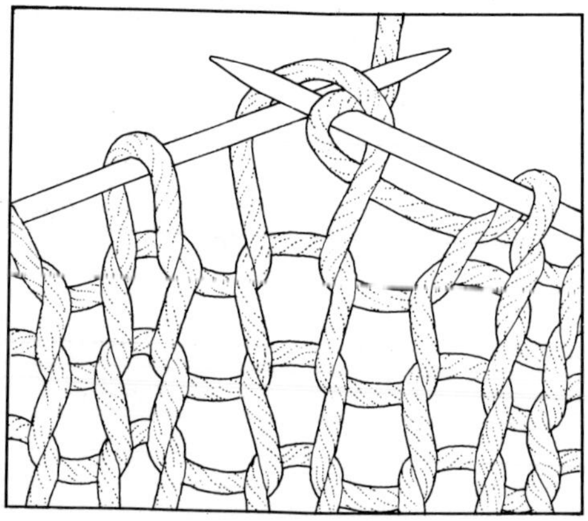

4 For the next row, hold the needle containing stitches in your left hand and begin again. The side of the work facing you while casting on and subsequently while making knit stitches is known as the 'knit side'. Continue until the full number of knit stitches in the instructions are completed. Take very great care with your counting. It is essential to get the foundations of a garment correct and even.

Purl Stitches

1 Hold the needle containing the cast on stitches in your left hand and pull the yarn to the front of your work – between you and the needles. (The yarn should still be wrapped around your right hand as previously instructed).

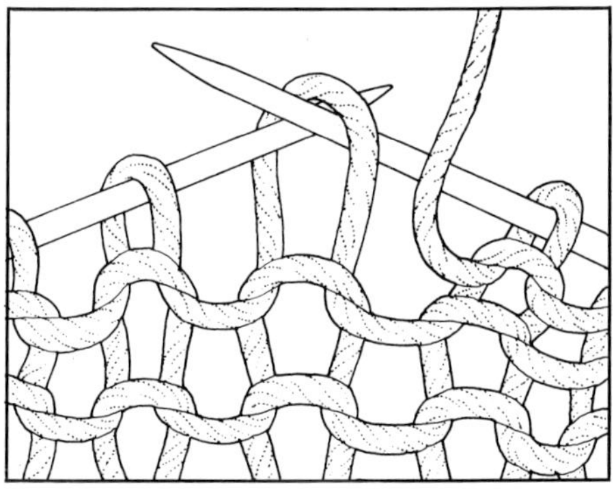

2 Now put the right hand needle through the front of the first stitch, from right to left.

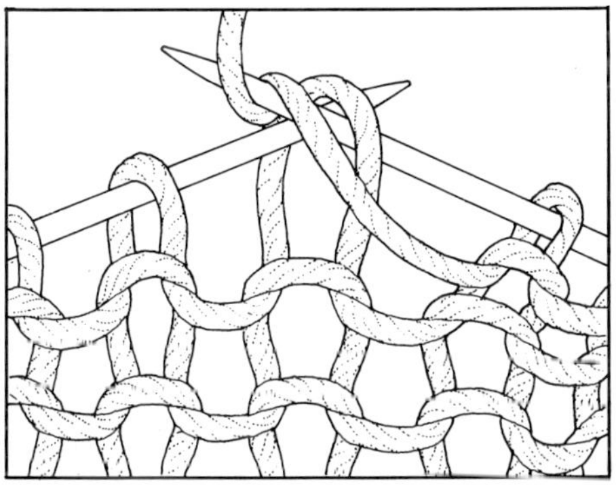

3 Take the yarn over the right needle, back behind the point and up. Then twist the right hand needle to pull the new loop through the old loop on the left hand needle and onto your right hand needle.

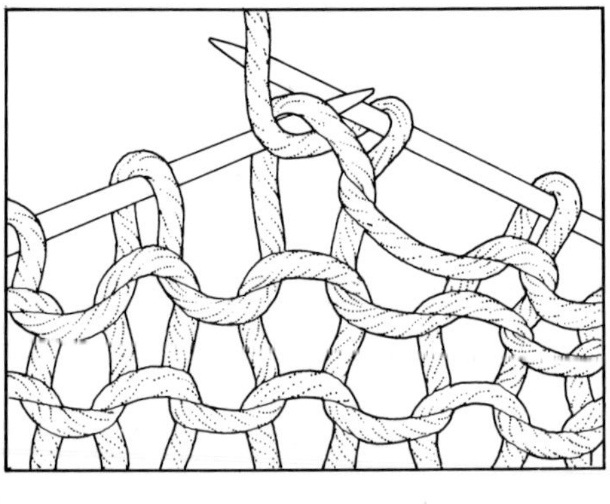

OTHER STITCHES

Garter Stitch

Knitting or purling every row backwards and forwards on two needles produces garter stitch, one of the oldest and smoothest of knitting effects.

Stocking Stitch

Knit one row, purl one row, knit one row.

Ribbing

Usually this consists of one or two knit stitches, followed by one or two purl stitches, to give the stretchable neatness required for cuffs and the bottom edge of sweaters that need to hug the hips.

Double Crochet

1 If necessary, first make a chain: make a slip loop on the crochet hook, then, holding the crochet hook in your right hand, twist the hook under and over the yarn to make another loop.

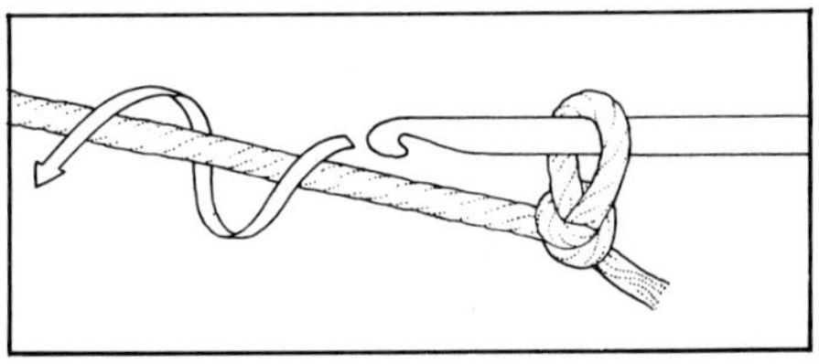

2 Pull the hook with the yarn through the first slip loop. Repeat.

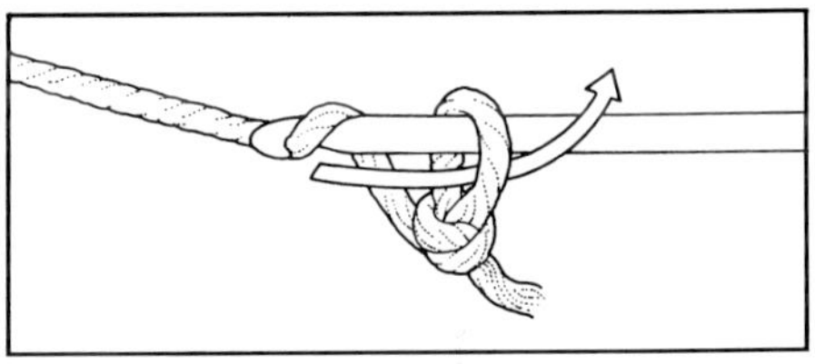

3 To double crochet, place the crochet hook into the second chain from the hook. Bring the yarn round, pulling one loop through so that two loops rest on the hook.

4 Bring the yarn around again and pull it through the two loops on the crochet hook.

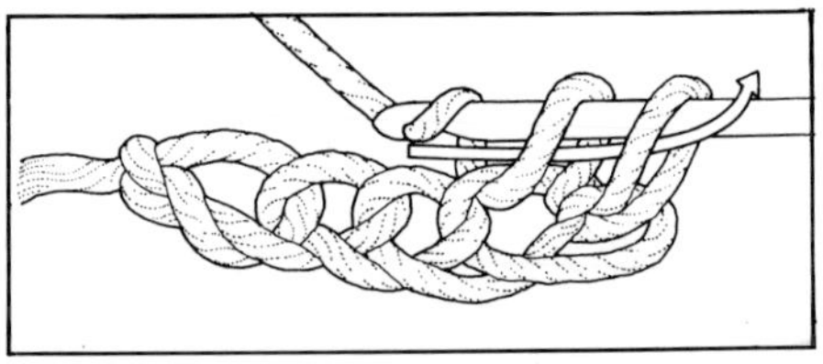

5 Repeat, working double crochets into the next and following chains to the end.

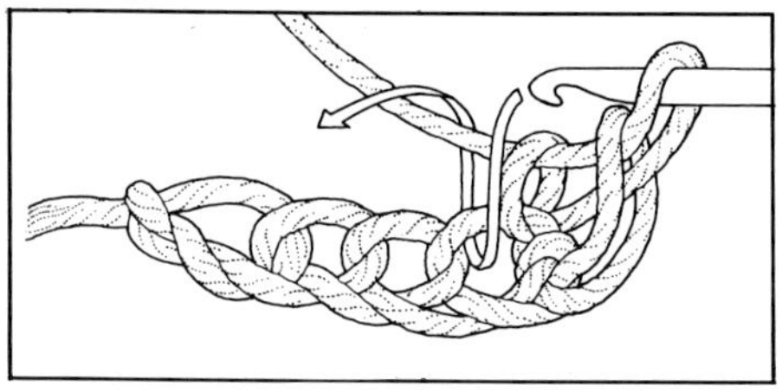

6 Make another chain, turn your work around, and begin again, placing the crochet hook in the first stitch of the row below.

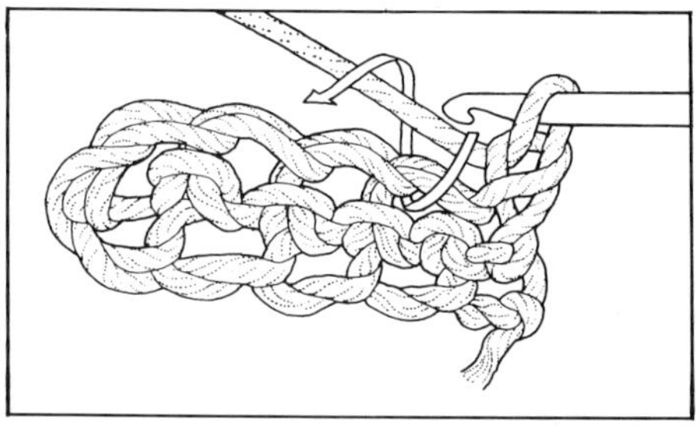

TENSION

Incorrect tension is the undoing of a good knitter. Many garments have turned out too tiny or too huge because of incorrect tension.

The tension is always given at the beginning of a pattern. It is shown as the number of stitches and the number of rows in a particular pattern i.e. 18 sts. and 26 rows garter stitch usually to 10 cm. (4 in.) square. The instructions also include the size of needles to be used.

The wrong size needles will produce the wrong size garment unless in the hands of a brilliant, experienced and innovative knitter.

Knit a tension sample and then check the measurement. A variation in tension is sometimes caused by a variation in the way you hold the yarn. A common habit is to hold the yarn with increasing tightness as you go along. Keep the way it is wound around your fingers exactly the same.

To check the tension of your sample, lay a small square of your work on a flat surface and, using a rigid ruler, check it against the measurement given. If there are more rows than there should be, you are holding the yarn too loosely, and if there are less, too tightly.

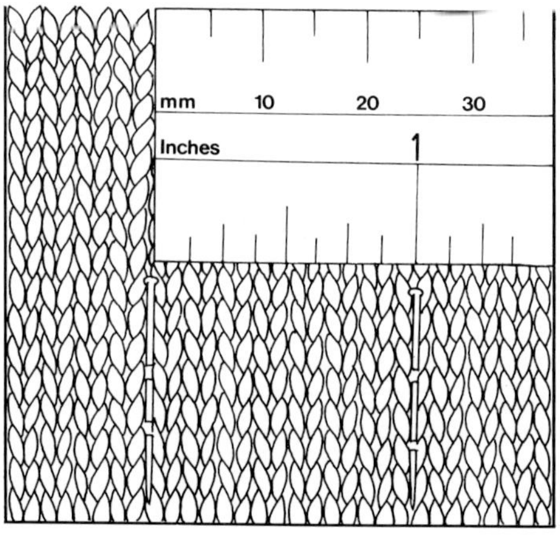

INCREASING

1 To increase one stitch on a knit row, knit into the front and then into the back of the same stitch, then slip the stitch onto the right hand needle.

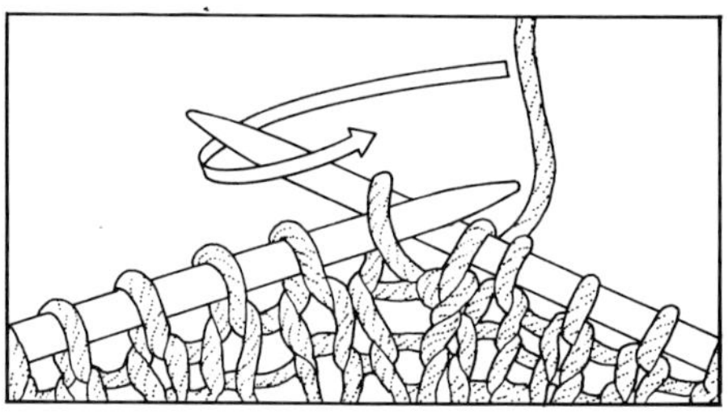

2 To increase one stitch on a purl row, purl into the front and then into the back of the same stitch, then slip the stitch onto the right hand needle.

DECREASING

1 To decrease one stitch on a knit row, place the right hand needle knitwise into the second and then the first stitch and knit together.

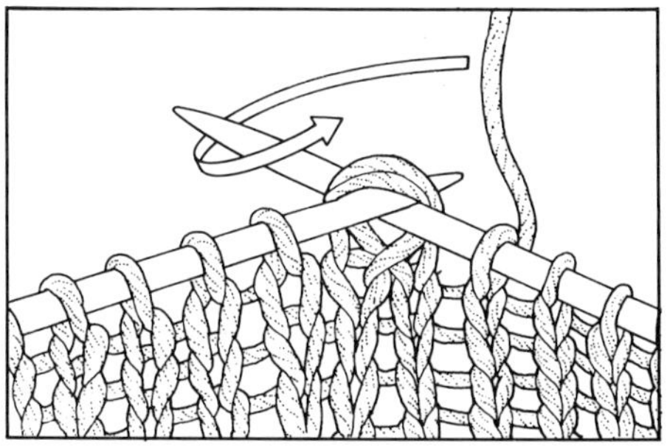

2 To decrease one stitch on a purl row, place the right hand needle purlwise through the first then the second stitch and purl together.

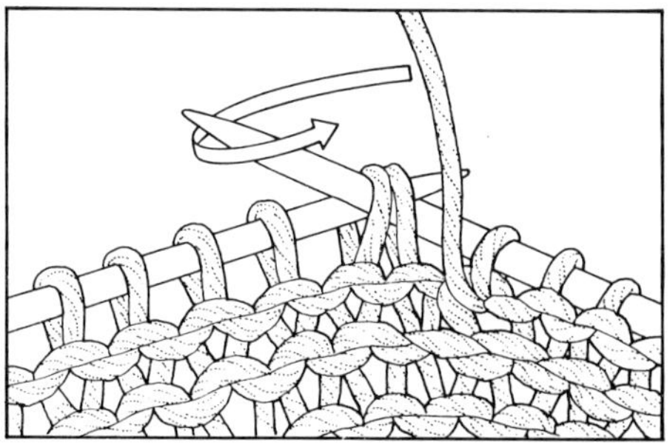

KEEPING COLOURS SEPARATE

When knitting with several colours, keep them apart by securing each ball of colour in an individual plastic bag tied firmly at the top with an elastic band.

BUTTONHOLES

The garment pattern details how and when the buttonholes are to be made. Hold the garment against you as you go along and check that the buttonholes are in the right place for you. The size of a buttonhole can be altered by adding or taking away stitches to be cast off (on the armhole edge) on a horizontal buttonhole, or by increasing or decreasing the number of rows worked for a vertical bottonhole. Check the button size with the buttonhole as you go along.

BEADS AND BUTTONS

Whatever the weight of your yarn, choose lightweight beads or buttons. Make sure they are colour fast. Wooden beads may be used for woollen knitting yarn and small, lustrous or gaily coloured ones with a lighter, cotton mix.

UNRAVELLING

If you do have to unravel, do it quickly and do it over the back of a chair. Wind the yarn around the back of the chair to keep it from getting tangled or stretched.

CASTING OFF

Knit rows

1 Knit the first two stitches, then place the point of the left hand needle through the first stitch.

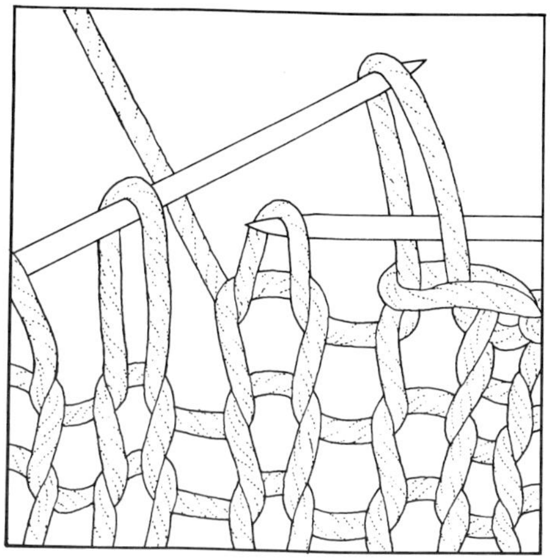

2 Draw the first stitch over the second stitch letting it fall. Repeat to the end of the row, knitting loosely.

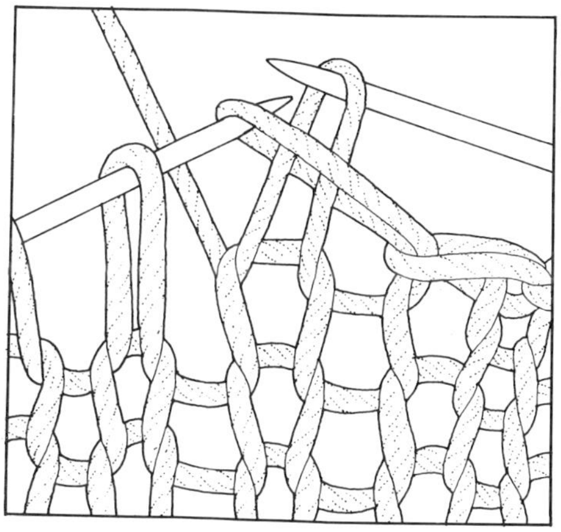

Purl rows

If casting off on a purl row simply purl the stitches instead of knitting them.

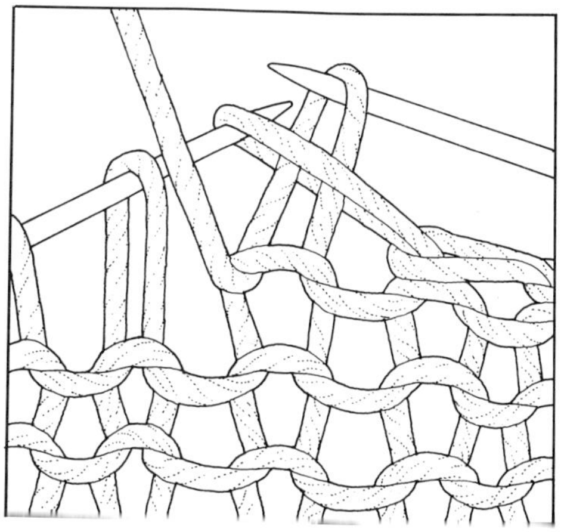

Ribbing

If casting off while ribbing, follow the pattern, casting off in both knit and purl.

FINISHING AND MAKING UP

Complete your final stitch and make use to leave at least 15 cm. (6 in.) of yarn from the end of the work. Draw the yarn through the last loop and tighten. Darn the end into the back of the work.

Pressing

Carefully check pressing instructions with each individual pattern. Certain pieces must be carefully pressed into shape before the garment is sewn up. When pressing is required, place the knitted pieces right side downwards onto a table covered with a smooth blanket. Press each piece with a damp cloth – excluding any ribbing – until all of the crinkles and curls are flat. Then wait for them to dry.

Lay the pieces alongside each other making sure that all the seams lie straight. Press again using a damp cloth and warm iron. Press the iron down onto the fabric and then lift up. Do not move the iron about over the knitted surface as this will stretch the pieces of the garment.

Embossed patterns should be pressed under a damp cloth, but take care not to flatten the pattern. If ribbing is to be pressed, press it very lightly and adjust it to the pattern while still warm.

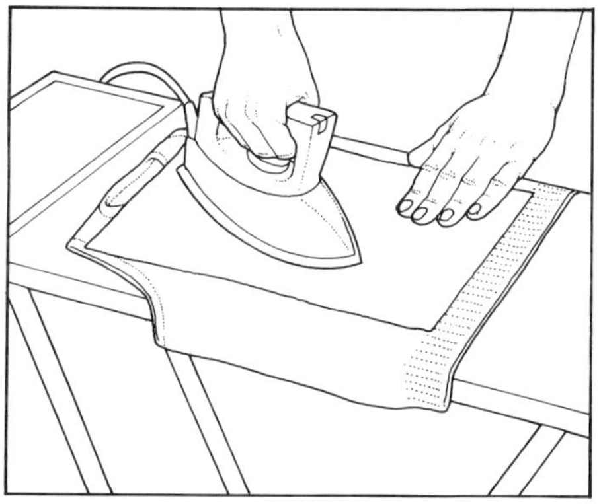

Sewing Seams

Sew up using the same coloured yarn and taking care to make the work neat but not drawn too tightly. Press again.

Seam Choice

For straight seams you can choose one of two methods – the edge to edge seam or the backstitch seam.

1 Edge to edge seam

On delicate knits this seam is almost invisible. Match the pieces to be joined edge to edge. Take a needle and matching yarn and stitch from one knit stitch 'head' to the alternate 'head' on the opposite piece.

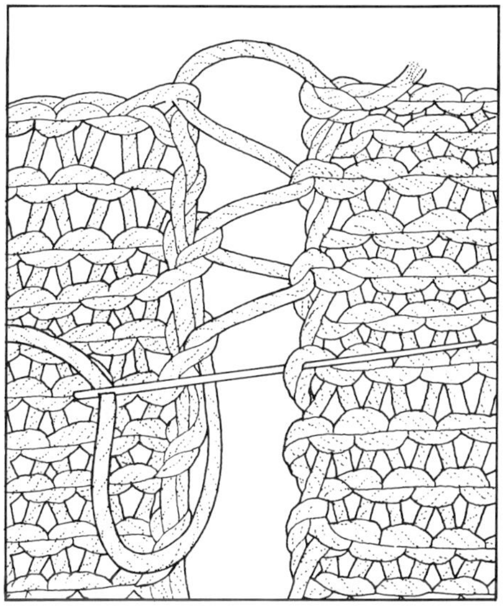

2 Backstitch seam

Put the pieces to be joined together, right sides facing. Match pattern to pattern, row to row and stitch to stitch. Back stitch along the seam sewing into the centre of each (to match the stitch on the other piece). Make the seam 6 mm. (¼ in.) from the edge of the knitting.

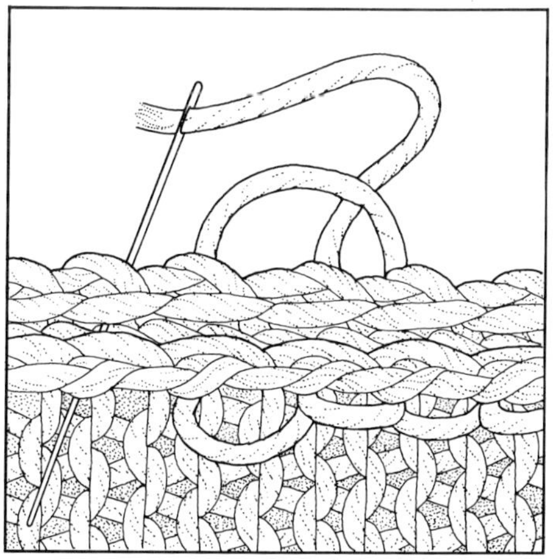

WASHING INSTRUCTIONS

1 Use mild soap and warm water (cold water if the colour is likely to run). Squeeze soap suds into the knitted garment gently then rinse well.

2 Place the knitted garment in a thick towel and roll it up tightly so that as much moisture as possible is absorbed.

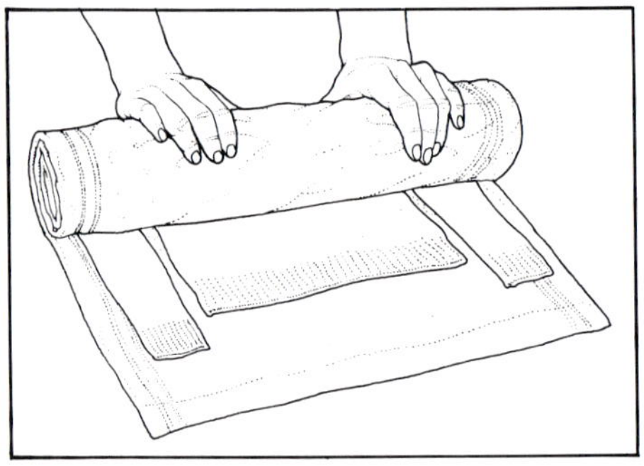

3 Lay the knitted garment out flat, neatly shaped on a dry, clean towel. Keep it away from direct heat. When dry the garment should be folded rather than hung up so that it does not lose its shape.

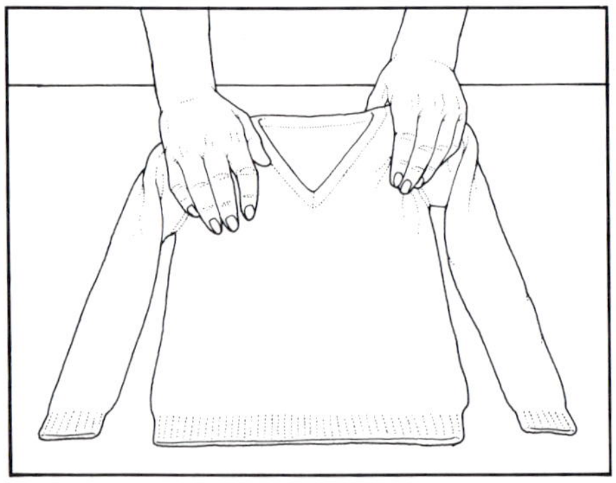

ABBREVIATIONS

alt.,	alternate
beg.,	beginning
C.,	Contrast shade
C.B.,	slip next 2 sts. on cable needle to back of work, k. 2, then k. 2 from cable needle
C.F.,	slip next 2 sts. on cable needle to front of work, k. 2, then k. 2 from cable needle
C.8F.,	slip next 4 sts. on cable needle to front of work, k. 4, then k. 4 from cable needle
cm.,	centimetres
cont.,	continue
d.c.,	double crochet
dec.,	decrease
foll.,	following
g.,	gram
g.st.,	garter stitch
in.,	inches
inc.,	increase, increasing
k.,	knit
k.b.,	knit into back of next stitch
k. 1 blw.,	knit 1 below, knit into next stitch one row below, at the same time slipping off stitch above
M. or MS.,	Main shade
m. 1,	make 1 by picking up and knitting into back of horizontal strand lying before next st.
m. 1k.,	make 1 knitways by picking up loop that lies between st. just worked and following st. and knitting into back of it
m. 1p.,	make 1 purlways by picking up loop that lies between st. just worked and following st. and purling into back of it
m.b.,	make bobble according to instructions in pattern
mm.,	millimetres
p.,	purl
p.s.s.o.,	pass slipped stitch over
patt.,	pattern
r.s.,	right side
rem.,	remaining
rep.,	repeat
rev.st.st.,	reversed stocking stitch
sl.,	slip
sl. 1k.,	slip one knitways
sl. 1 p.,	slip one purlways
st.st.,	stocking stitch
sts.,	stitches
t.b.l.,	through back of loops
tog.,	together
tw. 2,	knit next 2 sts. together but do not slip off left needle, now knit the first st. again slipping both sts. off needle
w.s.,	wrong side

READER SERVICE
We shall be happy to deal with your queries if you write to:
Patons & Baldwins Limited
16 St George Street
London W1R 9DE
Please enclose a ball band of the yarn specified, and a stamped addressed envelope.

For perfect results use the recommended yarns. Keep ball bands for washing and pressing instructions. Caution: it is essential to work in the stated tension, and Patons & Baldwins Limited cannot accept responsibility for the finished product if any other than the recommended Paton's Yarn is used.